The College Student's Research Companion

THIRD EDITION

Arlene Rodda Quaratiello

Neal-Schuman Publishers, Inc.
New York   London

Published by Neal-Schuman Publishers, Inc.
100 Varick Street
New York, NY 10013

Printed and bound in the United States of America

The paper used in this publication meets the minimum requirements of American National Standard for Information Sciences—Permanence of Paper for Printed Library Materials, ANSI Z39.48—1992 ∞

Library of Congress Cataloging-in-Publication Data

Quaratiello, Arlene R.
  The college student's research companion / Arlene R. Quaratiello.—3rd ed.
      p. cm.
  Includes index.
  ISBN 1-55570-477-8 (alk. paper)
  1. Library research—United States. 2. Report writing. I. Title.

Z710.Q37 2003
025.5'24—dc21

                                                    2003044534

Dedication

This third edition of *The College Student's Research Companion* is dedicated to my family's second addition, Julia, who slept so soundly while I wrote it.

REE: READ THE MAP: LIBRARY ORGANIZATION   37

The Lay of the Land   38
     The Dewey Decimal Classification   41
     The Library of Congress Classification   42

UR: STOP FOR DIRECTIONS:
   REFERENCE SOURCES   49

Encyclopedias: A Good Starting Point   51
     The Importance of Consulting the Index   52
     Subject-Specific Encyclopedias: Off the Main Drag   53
Dictionaries: What Do You Mean?   55
Atlases: Beyond Where   56
Statistical Sources: How Much? How Many?   57
Chronological Sources: When?   58
Biographical Sources: Who Are You?   60
Directories: Getting in Touch   62
Quotation Sources: Say What?   63
Bibliographies: Where Do I Go from Here?   64

VE: FIND YOUR WAY: PERIODICALS
   AND PERIODICAL INDEXES   65

Types of Periodicals   66
Indexes: Your Road Maps for Finding Articles   67
     A Basic Example of an Electronic Index   68
     Print Indexes   72
     Index Selection   74
Getting Your Hands on the Articles   75
     Formats   76
     Periodical Organization   77
     What If Your Library Doesn't Have It?   78

X: CHOOSE THE VEHICLE: SELECTING
   ELECTRONIC RESOURCES   81

Types of Access   81
Types of Databases   84
Popular Electronic Resources   85
     InfoTrac   86
     EBSCO*host*   87
     ProQuest   89

Contents

List of Figures and Tables
Preface

**ONE: START THE ENGINE: RESEARCH
ESSENTIALS**
Choosing Your Destination
Planning Your Trip
Types of Sources
Books
Periodical Articles
Web Sites
How and Where You Will Find These Sources
Using Other Libraries
Planning Your Time
About the Examples Used in This Book
Consider the Road Less Traveled

**TWO: HIT THE ROAD: THE ONLINE CATALOG
AND DATABASE SEARCHING BASICS**
The Structure of Online Catalogs
Searching Techniques
Searching by Title or Author
Searching by Subject
Searching By Keyword
Boolean Logic and Using the Connector A
Using the Connector OR
Truncation
Using the Connector NOT
Combining Connecting Terms
Problems with Keyword Searching
Field-Specific Searching

H.W. Wilson   90
FirstSearch   92
LexisNexis™ *Academic*   93
SilverPlatter and Ovid   96
Dialog@CARL   96
NetLibrary   98
"Free" Web Sites Worthy of Mention   99
    United States Government Databases   99
    Ingenta   101

**SEVEN: USE THE VEHICLE: SEARCHING
ELECTRONIC RESOURCES   105**

Accessing Databases   106
Searching Databases   106
    Subject Versus Keyword Searching   107
    Natural Language Searching   109
    Broadening Your Search   110
        Searching the Full Text   110
        Using OR and Truncation   111
    Narrowing Your Search   112
        Using Limiters   112
        Using AND and NOT   113
        Proximity Operators   113
        Field-Specific Searching   113
        Combining Field-Specific Searches   116
A Review of the Directions   117

**EIGHT: EXPLORE UNCHARTED TERRITORY:
THE WORLD WIDE WEB   121**

The State of the Web   121
The Structure of the Web   123
The Content of the Web   124
Finding Information on the Web   126
    Web Addresses   126
    "Surfing"   127
    Search Engine Overview   130
        Search Engine Directories   133
        What Are You Searching?   136
        Searching Techniques   137

Order of Web Pages Found 140
Search Engine Recommendations 141

**NINE: BRING IT ALL BACK HOME:
EVALUATING AND CITING INFORMATION** **143**

Evaluating What You've Found 143
Authority: Who Wrote It? 144
Content: Does It Adequately Address My Topic? 145
Accuracy: Is the Information Correct? 146
Currency: When Was It Written? 146
The Record of Your Trip: Citing Your Sources 148
Citing Books 149
Citing Periodical Articles 150
Citing Web Pages 152
Looking Back Down the Road 153
Epilogue: Riding Off Into the Sunset 155

Permissions **157**
Index **159**
About the Author **167**

List of Figures and Tables

FIGURES AND TABLES

Figure 2.1:   An example of an online catalog record.   18

Figure 2.2   An example of an online catalog's opening search screen.   19

Figure 2.3   A sample search form for searching an online catalog by title.   20

Figure 2.4   An example of a subject heading list in an online catalog.   22

Figure 2.5   A typical online catalog title display.   24

Figure 2.6   A sample listing in *The Library of Congress Subject Headings*.   25

Figure 2.7   Diagram representing a search for **women and drug abuse**.   30

Figure 2.8:   Diagram representing a search for **women and drug abuse and treatment**.   30

Figure 2.9:   Diagram representing a search for **air pollution or water pollution**.   32

Figure 2.10   Diagram representing a search for **drug abuse not alcohol**.   33

Figure 5.1   Opening search screen for InfoTrac's *Expanded Academic ASAP*.   69

Figure 5.2   Subject listing for **Mount Everest** in InfoTrac's *Expanded Academic ASAP*.   69

Figure 5.3   List of citations under the subject **Mount Everest** in InfoTrac's *Expanded Academic ASAP*.   70

Figure 5.4   Subdivisions of **Mount Everest** in InfoTrac's *Expanded Academic ASAP*.   71

Figure 5.5   Listing of citations under the heading **EVEREST, Mount** in *Reader's Guide to Periodical Literature*.   73

Figure 6.1   Opening search screen for EBSCO*host*'s *Academic Search Premier*.   88

Figure 6.2   Opening search screen for ProQuest.   89

Figure 6.3   Opening search screen for *Biography Plus* via WilsonWeb.   91

Figure 6.4   Opening search screen for OCLC's FirstSearch.   93

Figure 6.5   Opening search screen for LexisNexis™ *Academic*.   94

Figure 6.6   Opening search screen for SilverPlatter's *MLA Bibliography*.   95

Figure 6.7   Opening search screen for Ovid's *Sociological Abstracts*.   95

Figure 6.8   Homepage for Dialog@CARL.   97

Figure 6.9   An example of an "eBook" available via netLibrary.   98

Figure 6.10 The National Library of Medicine's homepage providing free access to *Medline*.   100

Figure 6.11 ERIC Database simple search screen.   101

Figure 6.12 GPO Access database list.   102

Figure 6.13 Ingenta homepage.   103

Figure 7.1   Records retrieved in EBSCO*host*'s *Academic Search Premier* for a search on **college campuses and binge drinking**.   108

Figure 7.2   Full record for an article in EBSCO*host Academic Search Premier*.   109

Figure 7.3   InfoTrac's keyword search mode.   111

Figure 7.4   Advanced searching in InfoTrac.   115

Figure 7.5   An advanced search for **drug** and **alcohol abuse** among **adolescents**.   117

Figure 8.1   A portion of a page from NASA's Web site.   127

Figure 8.2   A portion of a page from "The Nine Planets: A Multimedia Tour of the Solar System" by Bill Arnett.   128

Figure 8.3   Lycos homepage.   131

Figure 8.4   Google homepage.   132

Figure 8.5   Yahoo! homepage.   134
Figure 8.6   Yahoo! "Arts & Humanities" directory.   135
Figure 8.7   Yahoo! "Museums, Galleries, and Centers"
             directory.   136
Figure 8.8   Google advanced search page.   139
Figure 8.9   Lycos advanced search page.   140

Table 3.1   Dewey Decimal Classification.   40
Table 3.2   Library of Congress Classification.   43
Table 8.1   Tools for Searching the Web.   129–130

Preface

I remember how daunted I felt first walking into the library as a college freshman. The sight of all those books made me a bit dizzy (or maybe it was the awful dining hall food?). I wondered how I'd ever learn to find my way through the maze. At that time my research experience was on a par with the average college student (in other words, very little). I spent a fair share of time wandering aimlessly and wasting time unsure of where to start. Slowly I learned the ropes of research, learning to love the process, and eventually I went on to become a librarian. I wrote the first edition of *The College Student's Research Companion* in 1997 out of empathy for freshman and other students unfamiliar with academic libraries, I created a practical guide to give undergraduates a map to complete research competence. I even tried to make it fun.

Here's a true story. One research assignment in college required that I retrieve a book from the compact shelving for the first time. I opened the shelves successfully, but as I walked in to get the books, the shelves literally started closing in on me. The potential headline of the student paper flashed before my eyes: "Crushed in the Stacks!" Would my college career come to a sudden halt at that moment? Fortunately, I pushed the shelves apart long enough to escape. Although *The College Student's Research Companion* can't guarantee tips on quick escapes from dangerous shelving, I hope it helps prevent students from feeling "crushed" by their assignments.

I have aimed to create a "user-friendly" guide explaining the fundamental principles of academic library research.

These principles can be applied to all college libraries regardless of the size of their collections or the variety of their electronic resources. The basic research theories covered stand the test of time. This third edition of *The College Student's Research Companion* has been revised to reflect new developments in information technology. For example, since database providers and Web search engine companies are constantly changing their products, the most substantial changes have been made to Chapter 6, which describes the most popular electronic resources currently available in libraries, and Chapter 8, which covers searching the Web. I have revised the descriptions of databases available through InfoTrac, EBSCO*host*, and others, and added new resources like ingenta and netLibrary. Some Web search engines such as Snap.com and Northern Light have been dropped, while Google has been added. These are just some of the changes that have been made to enhance the usefulness of this book. How you use these resources, however, hasn't really changed substantially, so the underlying concepts about research emphasized in previous editions remain basically the same.

This third edition of *The College Student's Research Companion* continues to teach that information should be judged for what it conveys, not how it is conveyed—in other words, for its content rather than its format. As students increasingly turn to computerized resources, this philosophy is more relevant than ever. They need to understand the value of each search result—now available through many different resources. Perhaps an older article on microfilm may prove more valuable for a certain project than a recent article found through an online service; conversely, a search of the Web may indeed answer a question more effectively than the august, bound print materials available in a particular library. Selecting sources regardless of their format results in higher quality research and better research papers.

Even though the Web may appear to have made things easier, in actuality, the library (both real and virtual) has become an increasingly complicated place. This guide steers students through the labyrinth of resources available and takes them through the entire research process. They learn step-by-step, starting with the initial topic selection through to citing resources in a bibliography. It will teach all the necessary background skills to prepare a student for the task of writing a research paper.

An introductory chapter discusses topic selection and provides an overview of research. Chapter 2 explains how to use online catalogs, and Chapter 3 focuses on classification systems and how material is organized in libraries. This is followed, in Chapter 4, by an overview of print and computerized reference sources. Chapter 5 discusses how to find periodical articles using indexes in both electronic and print formats. The next two chapters, 6 and 7, focus on electronic resources: how to choose them and how to use them. Chapter 7, which covers advanced database searching techniques, can also be considered an extension of the earlier discussion of online catalog searching in Chapter 2. Chapter 8 is concerned with searching the Web, and the book wraps up, in Chapter 9, with a discussion of evaluating and citing resources.

For schools fortunate enough to have credit courses in library skills, *The College Student's Research Companion* can serve as a textbook. It can also help to alleviate the frustration of instructional librarians who struggle with "one-shot" lectures. Professionals realize that because of the ever-increasing complexities of information technology, there is barely time to touch upon essential principles in a single class period; it's even getting difficult to cover everything in a semester-long course. By reading selected parts of this book, students can come to library instruction sessions with a common background and make the most of the time available. They can continue to consult it on their own since there is only so much that can be discussed in class.

Throughout this guide, I draw many comparisons between doing library research and going on a road trip. This metaphor was inspired by my fond memories of the "extended study breaks" my college friends and I would often take to escape campus pressures. We'd hop in somebody's car and head off to some destination, whether to admire the fall foliage or go to the beach on a warm spring day. Although, superficially, a road trip and a research paper would seem to have nothing in common, as you'll see in this book there are some surprising similarities.

Research is a journey of discovery that can be just as exciting and stimulating as a trip to an unknown destination. Too many students are intimidated or bored by library research. This latest edition of the *The College Student's Research Companion* is intended to be a travel guide of sorts—a guide with an entertaining tone that will make the library (both real and virtual) a less intimidating place. With the techniques students will learn by reading this book, they can find their way in the unfamiliar surroundings of college libraries so that doing research will become a positive and enjoyable experience.

One

Start the Engine: Research Essentials

A freshman majoring in computer science is taking a sociology course to fulfill a requirement and has a paper due in about two weeks. The paper must discuss some aspect of human behavior and society. Having chosen a topic, he goes to the librarian at the reference desk in his college library for help:

Student: I'm writing a research paper about the Y2K bug and society's reaction to it in the late 1990s . . . you know, like the way everyone was worried that all the computers would crash on New Year's Eve because of the date turning to 2000, and people hoarded water and avoided getting on elevators at midnight and that sort of thing. And then I want to examine the actual effects and how it wasn't really so bad after all. Could you show me how to find information on this topic?

Librarian: That sounds very interesting. Let me show you the online indexes for finding articles and then we can check the catalog to see if there are any relevant books.

Another student, who is in the same class, reluctantly goes to the library two weeks later (the night before his paper is due) and hesitantly goes to the reference desk after wandering around the library aimlessly for some time:

Student: Um . . . I don't know how to use the library . . . I have a paper due tomorrow and I can't find anything . . . I tried surfing the Web in my dorm room but that was a waste of time. Where are the sociology books? My professor says I need scholarly articles too.

Librarian: Hmmm . . . do you have a topic? The first thing you have to do is choose a topic. I can help you then. Do you have any ideas?

Which student do you think will have more success in doing research and a more pleasant library experience?

CHOOSING YOUR DESTINATION

In my experience, the students who seem confused and overwhelmed by the idea of doing research are those who don't really know what they're looking for in the first place. Many students walk into the library with a paper assignment and no idea what to do next. The first thing you should do to avoid frustration in the library is clarify with your professor anything you don't understand about the assignment. Then you need to come up with a topic you can be enthusiastic about.

I believe the most crucial step in the research process is defining what it is you're looking for, just as you first choose a destination when planning a trip. This is necessary to give you a firm foundation. Both students mentioned earlier have been given the same assignment: to write a research paper on some topic relating to human behavior and society. The first student has selected a narrow topic to write about, probably something that holds some personal interest for him. He has a clear idea of where he's headed. The second student hasn't nailed down a topic yet, and so he has no idea what information he really needs. He thinks that if he goes to the library and browses through the section of books concerned with sociology, he'll find what he needs. But he's probably going to have a difficult time, especially since he's starting the night before the paper is due.

When selecting a topic, it's always wise to choose something that will engage your curiosity—something that will motivate you when the going gets rough. When you plan a trip, for example, you naturally are drawn toward a place that appeals to you. In the same way, pick a paper topic that appeals to you. Think about the discussions in your classes that were interesting, something you read in a textbook that you would like to pursue further, or just something of personal interest. Brainstorm ideas with your friends and classmates.

Even if you're not given a great deal of latitude in choosing a topic for a particular class assignment, you can come up with a "twist" that will make researching the assigned topic interesting. Relate it to something that does interest you. For instance, the first student in the previous example is really interested in computers. He's taking the sociology class to get a core requirement out of the way. So he relates the given assignment to computers. For another example— let's say you have to do a paper about some aspect of ancient Greek civilization. Unless you're a history or classics major, this assignment probably doesn't sound too thrilling at first. But perhaps you are interested in sports. How about doing some research on the ancient Olympic Games and the role that sport played in Greek society?

Once you feel that you have zoomed in on an interesting subject, take the following steps:

1) Write a brief statement of your topic. For example: "Society's overreaction to the Y2K bug in the late 1990s and its actual effects." This step is really quite simple. These topic statements might eventually serve as your paper's title.

2) Below this statement, write the major research questions that you'll want to answer, as well as some preliminary thoughts. To continue with our example, here are a few questions the student will need to address:

- What was the Y2K bug? How did it arise? Find out the history of the problem and how computer scientists went about solving it.
- Why were people apprehensive about it? Did it have anything to do with apprehension over the new millennium and society's overreliance on computers?
- How did people react? Find out more about the survivalist mentality; stocking up on provisions, refusal to fly or use elevators, abandoning use of computers, and so on.
- What were the actual effects of the Y2K bug? Compare the dire predictions with the actual outcome.

If you can write all of this down in a coherent manner, you'll have a clear understanding of your needs. The process of writing will also make your destination more concrete.

You don't have to pinpoint your topic to the minutest detail. In fact, if you're too narrow in your selection, you will limit yourself. Finding that balance between too broad and too narrow is an art that is often mastered through trial and error. You may find that once you start your research, your original topic will evolve into something different from what you had imagined. Something you come across in your reading may take you down another road. But such detours don't have to take you out of your way—in fact, they often take you on a shortcut to your ultimate goal.

Just remember, if you have no idea where you're going, you'll probably never get there. This holds true on the road as well as in the library.

PLANNING YOUR TRIP

After you've determined your topic, you are ready to map out your route. In other words, you should:

- identify the types of sources that will provide you with the information you need
- determine where and how you will find these sources
- estimate how much time you will need to do your research

Why should you have a plan? Well, without one, you'll probably end up wasting precious time browsing through the library. Although browsing can be effective in the preliminary phase of research by helping you select a topic and perhaps find some general information, it's not a very good method to use once you've chosen a topic—especially if your topic is very narrow. So think of browsing as a joyride—you have no particular destination but you may see some interesting things along the way. I have nothing against browsing—in fact, I love to browse. But I have observed some students who come in the day before a paper is due and try to get information by surfing the Web, flipping through issues of magazines, or wandering through a section of the library that seems to have books relating to their subject. This usually doesn't work very well.

Types of Sources

Books

When you think of a library, what's the first thing that comes to mind? Despite the prevalence of computers and electronic resources, books are probably what you picture first, and books do make up the bulk of just about all library collections. There are two main types of books in the library: circulating books—those you can check out, and reference books—those you must use within the library. These collections are generally kept in two separate areas of the building and are arranged by Library of Congress or Dewey Decimal call numbers.

Although a growing number of students seem to have developed an aversion to books and prefer to rely on electronic sources, nothing is likely to replace the book for depth of coverage as well as accuracy and authority of information. Books must go through a rigorous editorial process before being published. Facts must be checked and sources of information confirmed. While anyone can publish on the Web, you usually have to be considered an expert of some sort to have a book published. So if you want to gain a thorough knowledge of your topic, you must at least check to see if there are any relevant books. You don't have to read these books cover to cover; maybe there's just one pertinent chapter. Review the table of contents and index to determine which parts of a book to focus on.

The definition of a *book*, however, has become open to some interpretation in this electronic age. Some books are also published in electronic format—usually these are reference sources like encyclopedias, dictionaries, and handbooks, which are useful for obtaining quick and concise factual information on a broad range of topics, or classic works such as the *Bible* or *Moby-Dick*, which are no longer restricted by copyright and so are considered to be in the "public domain." In actuality, only a small number of sources originally published in book form are available on the Web. Many colleges now subscribe to a Web-based resource called netLibrary that provides the full text of over 40,000 books, still merely a sampling of the books available in print. If you don't have access to netLibrary, Project Gutenberg (at *promo.net/pg*) is another place you can go for electronic books. This site provides *free* access to over three thousand "public domain" titles.

Despite the growing popularity of netLibrary and similar resources, I think one reason electronic books are still relatively uncommon is the discomfort many people experience when reading computer screens for a long time. Books cover topics in depth and are, by nature, lengthy publications that require some patience and reflection on the part of the reader. Staring at a computer screen for the amount of time it takes to read a whole book can give some people a headache.

Electronic books are currently a novelty and you should not rely solely on these resources. Printed books still make up the vast majority of a library's collection, so don't overlook them.

Periodical Articles

Finding articles in periodicals is another essential component of doing research. Periodicals consist of any publication that comes out on an ongoing basis. As with books, there is generally some sort of editorial process that gives the material added validity. As any writer will tell you, it's easy to have an article rejected from a periodical and often takes a good deal of persistence to get published.

Types of periodicals include:

- newspapers
- popular magazines
- scholarly journals

The difference between popular magazines and scholarly journals will be discussed at greater length in Chapter 5. Although it is difficult to draw a line distinguishing the two, and the terms are often used interchangeably, the main difference is that when your professors require you to use journal articles rather than those in magazines, they mean to find publications of a more scholarly nature. The word *magazine* usually indicates a publication of a lighter sort for a more general audience, while the word *journal* is more often used when referring to an academic source. But the distinction can be blurry.

Sometimes periodicals provide the only useful information on very narrow or very current topics. For example, before the turn of the millennium, there were thousands of articles written about the dreaded Y2K bug but not many books, since the outcome was still uncertain.

Web Sites

When I refer to the Web as a source of information, I am not talking about the sources available on the Web that were originally published in other formats—namely, periodical articles that you can obtain through Web-based indexes or electronic books from subscription services like netLibrary. I am referring to sources unique to the Web. While evaluating the information you find in book and periodical sources has always been important, evaluating Web sites is crucial. As mentioned before, anyone can put anything on the Web. Sites often lack depth, authority, and accuracy. Although it's hardly the global electronic library it's hyped up to be by the media, there is a great deal of interesting material available on the Web, and it can a be a good source of quick information. However, proceed with caution.

Of course, a library provides more than just books, periodicals, and Web access. There are other types of informational resources: videotapes and DVDs, government documents, conference papers, dissertations, maps, photos, and other graphical material. Many libraries have special collections that may relate in some way to the college curriculum or local history. These resources often can't be pigeonholed into the broad categories above. Sometimes there is overlap and you will find references to these kinds of items while searching for books, periodicals, and Web sites. For example, some libraries include nonbook material in their online catalogs, while government documents are covered in various indexes.

How and Where You Will Find These Sources

Once you have pinpointed your informational needs, you'll require the means to fulfill these needs—just as you'd need a car to get to your destination. To do effective research, you have to know how to use the traditional library as well as the virtual one. In addition to knowing the basics of how libraries are organized, you will find it helpful to use online catalogs, electronic indexes, and Web search engines.

In the first part of this book, I'll explain how to use an online catalog most efficiently to find books and other library material on your topic. Since most online catalogs are now available on the Web, my examples will focus on searching Web-based catalogs. But even older forms of electronic catalogs operate according to similar procedures. From these catalogs, you obtain titles and call numbers. The next step is getting your hands on the items described in the catalog. Since most of the items included in online catalogs are books, I'll take you on a tour through the stacks—those rooms filled with shelves and shelves of books—and explain how everything is organized. Finally, I'll point out the most useful reference books for college students' research papers.

To find articles in periodicals, you don't just browse through issues of magazines or journals or surf the Web hoping to find the complete text of an article on your topic. You first need to select the appropriate index or indexes. Each index covers a different set of periodicals. There are indexes that cover broad ranges of subjects and others that focus on more narrow disciplines. Often there is a lot of overlap. Most indexes are available in electronic form, making them much easier to use than their print predecessors. But to find articles from periodicals published before the 1990s, you often have to rely on print indexes. There are many indexes from which to choose. You should become familiar with those available in your library and determine the most appropriate ones to find articles pertaining to your topic.

To find Web sites, you must know how Web search engines work. Surfing the Web, like browsing in the library, can be ineffective. Just as online catalogs enable you to find books, and periodical indexes help you find articles, search engines locate Web sites. The problem is that when you use these tools, which are far from perfect, you often find a lot of irrelevant material. Part of this is due to the amount of junk that is on the Web, part to ineffective use of the search engines, and part to the design of the tools themselves. To quote Forrest Gump, search engines are "like a box of chocolates, you never know what you're gonna get." You can't control the content of the Web or the way the search engines work, but you can learn to use them as effectively as possible.

Learning how to use all these resources isn't something you want to do right before a paper is due. You didn't learn how to drive a car for one particular trip. You learned to drive so you would have a practical skill for life. In this "information society" we live in, finding information is also a skill you must develop to be successful in life. So you should become familiar with the library even before your first assignment is given. Even if you don't have a particular project yet, stop by the library and get acquainted with it. Try out all the electronic resources. Practice using your library's computers by looking up a subject of personal interest. What's your favorite TV show? Look it up in the electronic indexes and see what critics have to say about it. Where would you like to go for spring break? See if the library has any books about this destination.

Don't be shy about asking librarians for help. Their job is to assist you with any questions you have and your tuition pays their salaries, so take advantage of their services. Go on a tour if one is being offered even if you think it might be a bore—you'll be glad you did later even if all you remember is the location of the most comfortable study space. If you are given the opportunity to go with one of your classes to an instructional session, don't choose that day to cut class—you'll be sorry when the rest of your classmates breeze through their research. Finally, of course, read the rest of this book. The time you invest now in learning how to navigate through the library will save you a great deal of frustration in the future.

Using Other Libraries

Planning your route will also involve decisions such as whether to use the resources of another library. Since not every library can buy every book or provide access to every periodical source, you may have to go elsewhere for the material you need, particularly if another college library has a special collection that relates to your subject. Many smaller academic libraries have limited budgets and select books based upon the academic programs of the school. So a college that specializes in technology will have a lot of science books, but maybe not such a great collection in literature and the fine arts. Your library might be a member of a consortium—a group of libraries in the same area that share resources. You can also get materials you need through interlibrary loan (ILL), a service, available at just about every library, that locates a hard-to-find book or article elsewhere in the country and delivers it to your library. This is a helpful service, but you have to allow at least a week or two for the material to arrive.

Planning Your Time

Another important aspect of the planning stage is determining how long you will need to do your research and complete you paper. Although waiting until the last minute is a common practice, you should expect to be particularly stressed if you do this. The research process is a time-consuming one, no matter how many timesaving hints I give you.

There are two phases to completing a research paper: doing the research and writing the paper. Too often, students dismiss the research process as that boring task they have to get over with in the beginning. Research is a major component of a research paper; that's why it's called a *research* paper, and why I've written an entire book about doing research papers that focuses on research rather than writing.

Without material, you have nothing to write about. Good research results in papers that will get high marks from your professors. I believe it should take one-third to one-half of your time to do the research, depending on how adept a writer you are.

Although computers are a tremendous aid, they don't just spit out the exact information you need without some mental effort on your part. And you usually can't get all the information you need on a computer screen. Although an increasing number of computer databases provide the text of articles on screen and electronic versions of entire books are available on the Web, you'll most likely have to get your hands on some of the material you need. This requires time and effort.

The length of the paper as well as your own research experience will, of course, determine when you should start your research. I have no mathematical formula to offer concerning how many days you'll need to complete a certain number of pages. My primary recommendation is that you allow yourself time for roadblocks along the way: A book you need has been checked out; you realize that you'll have to go to another library or get a book through interlibrary loan; the computer system has crashed—there are any number of scenarios. Sometimes your gut instincts tell you when it's time to start. A mild anxiety may come over you. Since the cure for worry is action, just getting started will make you feel better.

Set aside a short time for an initial visit to the library well in advance of your paper's due date. Promise yourself you'll spend an hour on your research, but don't put any pressure on yourself. You don't even have to be successful in finding anything. Just go. Chances are you will have positive results. Then go again the next day. Spend some time each day working on your research. Take small steps and you'll see that slowly everything will come together. This really works—in fact, it's the approach I took in completing this book.

ABOUT THE EXAMPLES USED IN THIS BOOK

The car in which you learned to drive may not be the car you drive now. But because all cars operate according to the same principles, you'll find that things are fundamentally the same: You put your foot on the gas pedal to make the car accelerate or on the brake to slow down or stop; you turn the wheel to steer. Sure, little things are different: On a dark night when it starts to rain and you're borrowing a friend's car, you may have to search frantically for the windshield wiper controls or defroster. And you'll probably need a few extra lessons to learn how to drive a standard transmission if you're accustomed to automatic. In the future, perhaps, as you sit behind the wheel of your flashy new electronic automobile, you might look upon the car you drove in driver's ed as an antique, but the lessons you learned in that gas-powered vehicle should still be easily transferable.

The examples used in this book can be like that driver's ed car. Although you may not use exactly the same resources in your library, the examples I have chosen demonstrate fundamental principles that will enable you to use the particular resources that are at your disposal.

It is unavoidable that the sources I cover in the rapidly changing world of information technology will undergo minor as well as drastic modifications by the time you read this book. But I believe that most of these changes will be superficial, just as the look and performance of cars has been altered over the years but the way you drive them hasn't changed much. That's why it's so important to understand the basic theories of doing research rather than the specifics.

Perhaps you have had the disconcerting experience of visiting a Web site one day and returning the next to find that the site looks completely different or is gone altogether. Computers are constantly being upgraded and—supposedly—improved, but this leaves the average user feeling confused and a bit intimidated. My purpose, therefore, in using certain examples will be to demonstrate the fundamentals that endure, rather than give you specific instructions that might change by next week. With the knowledge of the underlying theories, you will have a road map that will lead you through unfamiliar territory.

CONSIDER THE ROAD LESS TRAVELED

A final point I would like to make before proceeding concerns how you choose resources; this point also relates to my discussion of books earlier in this chapter. Computers have certainly revolutionized the library. Electronic periodical indexes, multimedia reference sources, and the World Wide Web have changed the way research is done in countless ways. Some of these changes are good, but others, in my opinion, are not. The main problem that has arisen with the emergence of computerized resources is that many students have come to rely exclusively on computers. These students ask questions like "Why read a book?" and "Why track down old journal articles on microfilm?" I counter by asking, "Why limit yourself?" There is still plenty of information that is not available electronically and may never be. You should choose your resources based on content rather than format; in other words, judge a resource for its informational value rather than whether or not it's available on the computer.

This issue reminds me of a road trip I took with a friend of mine in Arizona. One beautiful spring afternoon, we drove off to "get our kicks on Route 66," the first highway constructed between Chicago and California back in the 1920s. It remained the major east-west route until the superhighway Interstate 40 was built parallel to it in the 1970s. Now Route 66 has become a byway, a back road that is traveled by tourists who have time to sightsee rather than drivers who are in a hurry to get somewhere. With all its roadside pit stops, hamburger joints, neon signs, teepees, ghost towns, and other quirky attractions, Route 66 is a much more interesting road to travel than I–40, which looks like just about every other superhighway in America.

Similarly, computerized resources have paved a super-highway through our libraries. Traditional resources remain but are often overlooked. As you read this book and use the techniques discussed in it, keep in mind that the best resources might not be the easiest to get. It may take you a little more time to find that obscure journal article or book, but it may well be worth it. Remember what Robert Frost wrote: "Two roads diverged in a wood, and I—I took the one less traveled by, and that has made all the difference."

Two

Hit the Road: The Online Catalog and Database Searching Basics

We will start our journey into the wonderful world of research by learning how to use the online catalog because this is the tool you use to find books, and as I said in the last chapter, books are usually the first things you associate with libraries. Remember, however, that online catalogs include other material besides books, such as CDs, DVDs, and videotapes. Searching the online catalog is similar to searching any computerized database, whether it be a periodical index for finding articles or a Web search engine for finding Web sites. So what I explain here will certainly carry over into other chapters of this book. Since the vast majority of online catalogs are now available via the Web, the examples in this chapter will use a generic Web catalog that should reflect whatever system you will use in your library, even if it is an older one.

Because you will probably need to search the catalogs of other libraries at some time, which can easily be done on the Web, it is useful to understand the basics that underlie all systems. The catalog of another library may be just a mouse-click away. There is also the possibility that your library—especially if you're at a small school—is part of a consortium and shares its catalog with other libraries in the area.

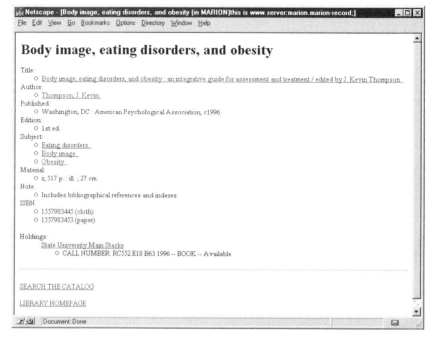

Figure 2.1: An example of an online catalog record.

THE STRUCTURE OF ONLINE CATALOGS

Each book in a particular library has a *record* in the online catalog (there may also be records for periodicals, videos, and so on). Figure 2.1 is an example of a record for a book. All of these records together comprise the *database* of what the library has—the library's "holdings."

Just as a database is composed of individual records, each record is composed of individual elements called fields. A *field* is a certain type of information about the item. For a book, such as the one in Figure 2.1, there are fields for the title, the author, and the publisher. Other essential fields include the subject field, which I will be discussing at great length in this chapter, and the call number, which is essential for getting your hands on the item. I will spend the entire next chapter explaining that.

Figure 2.2: An example of an online catalog's opening search screen.

SEARCHING TECHNIQUES

Although the layout and format of the online catalogs of different libraries may vary, fundamentally they all operate in the same way. There are four basic ways of finding books: by title, by author, by subject, and by keyword. Figure 2.2 displays a sample opening Web page for an online catalog. By clicking on any of the options on this screen, you will access the appropriate Web page that will provide a form for entering your search criteria. As you can see, it is often possible to search by numbers such as call number or ISBN (international standard book number), but usually this feature is used only by librarians.

Some online catalogs now make their default search screen a keyword search screen, which means that the computer will automatically do a keyword search for whatever terms you enter. So make sure you know what kind of search you are performing when you enter terms. You may have to click on a link or select an option from a pull-down menu in order to do a title, author, or subject search.

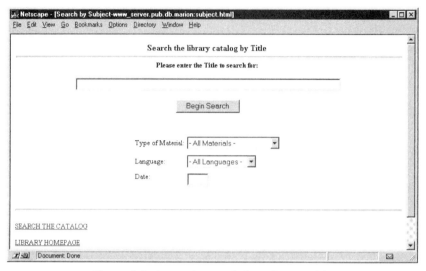

Figure 2.3: A sample search form for searching
an online catalog by title.

Searching by Title or Author

It is easy to find a book if you know the author's name or the exact title. Figure 2.3 displays a typical search form for title searching. You simply enter your title in the box and click "Begin Search." You can also easily limit the search to type of material (books or nonbooks), language (most useful for eliminating foreign language works), and date. This is a common feature of Web-based catalogs. If your library belongs to a consortium of libraries, the catalog may also allow you to limit by location.

There are a couple of simple rules that are commonly used when searching for books by author or title:

- When looking up an author, use the last name first. example: **King Stephen** (usually no comma is necessary)
- When looking up a title, the general rule is to drop any articles (although many catalogs will now just ignore a, an, and the).

Example: *A Tale of Two Cities* should be entered *Tale of Two Cities*.

If you do not find what you're looking for, first make sure you have followed these two rules, then check to make sure you have the correct spelling and the author or title you have entered is a valid one. The computer cannot read your mind; contrary to popular belief, it is just a stupid machine that takes all the commands you give it quite literally. By the way, you can usually type in your terms in lowercase.

Searching by Subject

Before searching for a book by subject, it is helpful to have a clear idea of your topic. As discussed in the preceding chapter, you'll wander aimlessly if you don't know where you're going. While your topic may evolve as you proceed, you do need to have some sense of direction.

Finding a subject heading that you can use is often a process of trial and error. But it's worth the effort. Despite the apparent ease of keyword searching, as I will explain in the next section, there is no better way to retrieve a complete list of relevant material than by subject searching. We can only hope that someday there will be a system for subject searching the Web as there is for library catalogs. We'll discuss this in more detail later in the book, but part of the reason you retrieve so much junk when using Web search engines to find Web sites is precisely because there are no subject headings assigned on the Web. Because of subject searching, online catalogs can be much more efficiently searched than the Web.

Here's an example of searching the online catalog by subject. Let's say you were doing a paper on eating disorders. Your first inclination would probably be to enter the subject heading **Eating disorders**. If you do this, you will certainly find books if your library has any on the topic because this is a valid heading. After clicking on the search button, you

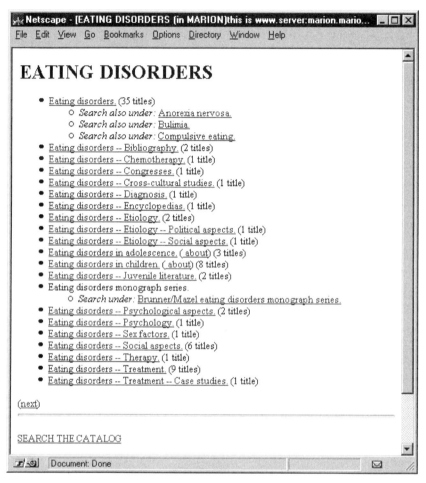

Figure 2.4: An example of a subject heading list in an online catalog.

will see subject headings similar to those listed on the screen displayed in Figure 2.4.

In this example, 35 books have been located on the general topic of eating disorders. However, the three lines below this heading—**Anorexia nervosa**, **Bulimia**, and **Compulsive eating**—offer what are known as *cross references*. Cross references are often narrower topics that fall under the main subject area, but they can also stand alone. By clicking the appropriate heading, you can perform a separate search for these subjects.

Below the cross references are *subheadings*. These are also narrower topics under the main heading, but they subdivide the main heading and cannot stand alone. **Eating disorders—Bibliography** and **Eating disorders—Encyclopedias** denote specific types of books; **Eating disorders—Etiology** denotes a subdivision of the main topic, in this case the study of the causes of eating disorders. This is further divided with sub-subheadings into political and social aspects.

Once you have found the appropriate subject heading, you are not finished because your goal is to get your hands on some books on the topic. You must delve to the next level to find the individual book records by clicking on the heading you want. This brings up a list of the individual books and other items as shown in Figure 2.5.

This screen gives you some basic information on each item: the author, title, publisher, and year. The location of the item is also indicated as well as its availability. The book may be available, checked out, or have some other status such as noncirculating (a reference book, for example) or on hold.

If you want to see complete records such as the one displayed in Figure 2.1, you need to select a particular title. I recommend that you take a look at some of the full records for one very important reason. If you look closely at Figure 2.1, you'll notice that the book retrieved has two other subject headings in addition to **Eating disorders**. These are **Body image** and **Obesity**. These subjects could be related to your research topic, so you might be interested in following them further. You can easily do this using a Web-based catalog. Simply click on the subject heading. By clicking the link for **Body image**, you will instantly retrieve the records for all the books on this subject. This is a powerful feature that gives you the ability to explore related material in a convenient manner.

Figure 2.5: A typical online catalog title display.

Subject searching doesn't always work as effortlessly as the previous example might suggest. Sure, **Eating disorders** is a subject heading, but not everything you might think to enter is going to be a heading. It's the same as when you look up a listing in the yellow pages and find that doctors aren't listed under **Doctors** but under **Physicians**. Subject headings are determined by the Library of Congress, which puts together the official list of standard, acceptable headings under which all library material is categorized. The print version of the list is actually quite long, contained in four big red books known as *The Library of Congress Subject Headings*, or, simply, the "red books." There is a Web-based version of the list now but it is available for use only by librarians.

Television advertising *(May Subd Geog)*
    [HF6146.T42]
    UF Advertising, Television
        Commercials, Television
        Television commercials
        Television in advertising
    BT Advertising
        Broadcast advertising
        Radio advertising
        Television broadcasting
    RT Television commercial films
    NT Cable television advertising
        Singing commercials
— **Awards** *(May Subd Geog)*
— — **United States**
        UF Television advertising—United
            States—Awards
            [Former heading]
        NT Clio Awards
— **Law and legislation** *(May Subd Geog)*
    BT Advertising laws
— **United States**
— — Awards
        USE Television advertising—
            Awards—United States
Television advertising and children
    (May Subd Geog)
    BT Children
Television advertising directors
    (May Subd Geog)
    [HF6146.T42]
    BT Television—Production and direction
Television advertising films
    USE Television commercial films
Television anchors
    USE Television news anchors
Television and baseball *(May Subd Geog)*
    UF Baseball and television
    BT Baseball
Television and children *(May Subd Geog)*
    UF Children and television
    BT Children
Television and copyright
    USE Copyright—Broadcasting rights

Figure 2.6: A sample listing in *The Library of
Congress Subject Headings.*

If you take the time to leaf through the pages of the "red books," they can help you determine appropriate headings to enter in the online catalog. It's also useful to review the structure of this list even if you don't ever use it, because it will give you a better understanding of how subject headings work. In this alphabetically arranged list, official headings are indicated by bold type. **Television advertising** is one such heading as displayed in Figure 2.6.

What does all this mean?

UF—**use for**—terms that **Television advertising** should be used for. This part isn't too useful, basically telling you, for example, that **Television advertising** should be used instead of **Television commercials**. Conversely, however, if you had looked up **Television commercials**, you would have been told to **USE Television advertising**— this *is* helpful.

BT—**broader term**—terms that will retrieve more material or material that covers a broader subject area. For example, **Broadcast advertising** will find material that covers advertising on both television and radio, so you'll probably find more books if you use it or books that have a wider scope of information.

RT—**related term**—suggestions for other terms you could try; in this example, **Television commercial films**.

NT—**narrower term**—terms that will limit your search. If you look up **Cable television advertising** or **Singing commercials**, which are narrower more specialized subjects, you will find fewer books.

Below all of this begins the list of subheadings you can use with **Television advertising**, which includes **Awards, Law and legislation**, and **United States**.

The online catalog will often perform the same function as the "red books," referring you to official headings as well as associated headings. Let's say you were looking for books about the Vietnam War. You'd probably just enter the subject heading **Vietnam War**. Having done this, however, you would see the following reference in our hypothetical catalog: **Vietnam War, 1961–1975** *search for* **Vietnamese Conflict, 1961–1975**. In a Web catalog, cross references are links to other Web pages so you could just click on **Vietnamese Conflict** and easily perform the right search. Although it seems a bit odd that the official heading is **Vietnamese Conflict**, it's not surprising when you remember that the Library of Congress is a branch of the United States Government. Since the Vietnam War was never officially recognized as a war, this is not an acceptable subject heading. But when was the last time you heard someone refer to the "Vietnamese Conflict?" If you search the online catalog for *titles* that contain that phrase you probably won't find any, but the majority of books on the topic will contain the phrase "Vietnam War" in their title.

You might also notice an occasional lack of political correctness in subject headings. For example, **Indians of North America** is the official heading for Native Americans. The wheels of the Library of Congress, as with any large bureaucratic institution, move slowly. Headings do change to reflect the times. **Moving picture plays**, for instance, was eventually changed to **Motion pictures**. But you are less likely to find terms in current usage established as subject headings. **Generation X** was only recently added to the list; before that, the term **Baby busters** defined that concept.

Sometimes subject searching can be downright infuriating. If you entered **Motion picture violence**, which is not a subject heading, you would be informed that there are no books on this subject. Often just changing the word order or playing around with the phrase a bit will do the trick. For example, you will find that **Violence in motion pictures** is a valid heading.

Another suggestion is to think of synonyms for your heading. Perhaps, considering the formality of Library of Congress subject headings, you might think to enter **Daytime dramas** to find books on soap operas, when, in fact, the official heading *is* **Soap operas** despite the colloquial sound of that term.

Searching by Keyword

Have you ever seen an old card catalog? Well, if not, it had a lot of little drawers in which index cards were filed alphabetically under the last name of every author and the first word of every title and subject heading of every book in the library. It took up a lot of space and could be a bit unwieldy to use. Now, imagine that cards could be added for each word contained in the titles, authors' names, and the subject headings—not just the first word or last name. In addition, imagine that the space on the cards is without limit, so summaries and notes could be added to the descriptions of many of the items and additional cards could be added and alphabetized under each word in these summaries and notes. The card catalog might possibly be bigger than the library building itself! Although even more unwieldy to use, this imaginary card catalog would enable you to find more books than you would have found the conventional way.

Here's an example. Suppose you are looking for books about headhunters (the kind that can get you a job, not the kind you often see on reruns of that classic '60s sitcom *Gilligan's Island*). If you pull out the appropriate *H* drawer in this massive, imaginary card catalog, you would find cards for books about both varieties of headhunters. But *My Friends, the New Guinea Headhunters* certainly won't serve your purpose. Before this, however, is a card for *How to Answer a Headhunter's Call: A Complete Guide to Executive Search*—again the word *headhunter* is in the title. Since the subject heading under which this book is officially categorized is **Executives—recruiting**, doing a traditional subject search would never have located it, but this keyword search does. You can do this sort of thing with an online catalog or just about any other searchable electronic database.

Keywords are words that appear anywhere in a computerized item record. A keyword can be in the title field, the subject field, the notes field—just about any field. You can search for single words or phrases, as well as combinations of words and phrases. It is best to avoid using common prepositions and articles such as *the*, *of*, *to*, and the like, which are called stopwords, as well as three special terms *and*, *or*, and *not*, which serve a special function to be discussed shortly.

Boolean Logic and Using the Connector AND

The real power of keyword searching is demonstrated when you need to look up more than one word or phrase. For example, let's say you can't remember the exact title of the book you need about how to deal with change, but you know that the author's first name is Spencer and you're positive that the word *cheese* is in the title. You enter the keyword search **spencer and cheese**, and through the magic of keyword searching you are able to locate *Who Moved My Cheese?* by Spencer Johnson. You have basically instructed the computer to find all the records that contain both terms.

Keyword searching using more than one term or phrase, such as in the previous example, operates according to the principles of Boolean logic, which were developed by George Boole, a nineteenth-century mathematician. These principles are quite straightforward. Boolean logic can be used to define a topic very specifically, so that from among millions of items in a library you can find the ones that meet your needs. The principles I'll discuss here are extremely important because they form the basis of searching any computerized database as well as using Web search engines effectively.

Keyword searching is invaluable for finding material on multidisciplinary subjects that are difficult if not impossible to define by one single subject heading. Suppose you wanted books about drug abuse among women. To understand Bool-

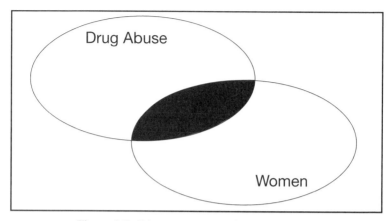

Figure 2.7: Diagram representing a search for
women and drug abuse.

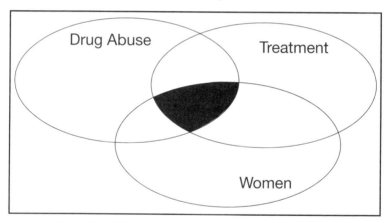

Figure 2.8: Diagram representing a search for **women
and drug abuse and treatment**.

ean logic, picture two sets of books: The first contains all
the books about women, and the second contains all the
books about drug abuse. A third set is formed by the books
that belong in both sets because they're about both women
and drug abuse. When the linking term AND is used, records
that contain the two words specified are retrieved. Figure 2.7
illustrates what is happening.

The portion of this diagram in black is the set representing records that include the terms **women** *and* **drug abuse**. The more terms you link together, the narrower your search becomes and the fewer records you will retrieve. For instance, a search for **women and drug abuse and treatment** will retrieve a narrower set, as in Figure 2.8.

The portion of this diagram in black is the set representing records that include the terms **women** *and* **drug abuse** *and* **treatment**. Notice that it is smaller than the highlighted portion in Figure 2.7.

If you don't find any books, or if you find only a few, you can try dropping a term. This will broaden your search. Or, if you get too much, narrow your search by adding a term. You will find that keyword searching can often be a process of trial and error like subject searching or finding your way around an unfamiliar area without a map.

Using the Connector OR

You can also use the word OR between terms to broaden a keyword search. Picture a set containing all the books about air pollution and another set containing all the books about water pollution. Some of these books may certainly overlap in subject material covering both topics. But the set resulting from a search for **air pollution or water pollution** will contain not only the books that address both topics, but also those that are about one or the other.

In Figure 2.9, the area in black represents those books that address both topics, but the areas in gray are also included in the resultant set because the connecting term OR was used. If you were to add another term to this search using OR, the outcome would be even larger because the more terms you link together with OR, the broader your search becomes; this is the opposite of what happens when using AND.

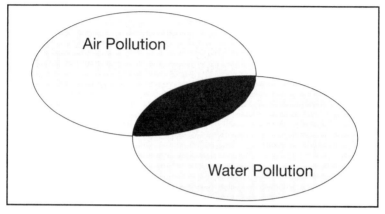

Figure 2.9: Diagram representing a search for **air pollution or water pollution**.

Truncation

Truncation can serve a purpose similar to that of OR. With this technique, available in many online catalogs, you drop the ending of a word and replace it with a truncation symbol. This symbol differs among catalogs and other computerized databases. The question mark (?), asterisk (*), and pound sign (#) are frequently used. For example, you could enter **environment?**, which would retrieve all of the records containing any words beginning with *environment*; in addition to *environment* itself, you would also retrieve *environments*, *environmental*, *environmentalists*, and so on. Occasionally no symbol is necessary and truncation is automatic.

Truncation is helpful when you want to retrieve both the plural and singular forms of a word; just substitute the catalog's truncation symbol for the "s." You can also use truncation symbols within words. For instance, if you wanted to find either **woman** or **women**, you might be able to enter **wom?n**, which would serve the same purpose as the lengthier **woman or women**. Once again, truncation is a feature not limited to online catalogs. It is an important con-

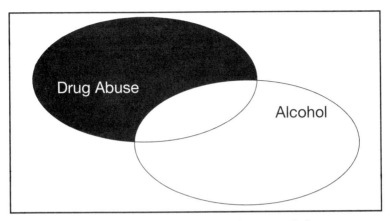

Figure 2.10: Diagram representing a search for
drug abuse not alcohol.

cept to understand when searching many computerized databases.

Using the Connector NOT

You can use the word NOT between terms to eliminate irrelevant items. For example, if you wanted to find all the books about drug abuse, but weren't interested in those dealing with alcohol, you could enter the search as **drug abuse not alcohol**. This would eliminate all the records in which the word *alcohol* appears, as Figure 2.10 illustrates.

In this figure, the area in black again represents the resultant set, but it is not a part of both original sets, only the set of books about drug abuse. Although NOT is used less often than the other two connecting terms, it can be helpful in avoiding one of the pitfalls of keyword searching—retrieving irrelevant records.

Combining Connecting Terms

You can combine ANDs, ORs, and NOTs in one search to get really specific. Although my examples here will involve using parentheses, many Web-based catalogs simplify the process with advanced search entry forms. What's important to understand is the theory behind this technique of combining search terms. Using parentheses when combining sets, or entering them separately in the boxes on a search form, defines your search criteria so the computer can sort them out correctly. The computer will do the search in parentheses first, and then combine the resultant set with the other terms.

For example:

> **(drug abuse not alcohol) and women**
> retrieves records concerning drug abuse among women, but not alcohol abuse

> **children and violence and (motion pictures or television)**
> retrieves records about the effects of violence in both movies and TV upon children

If I searched for **drug abuse not (alcohol and women)** instead of **(drug abuse not alcohol) and women**, I wouldn't find any books on women because the NOT eliminates both words inside the parentheses. **(Children and violence and motion pictures) or television** will retrieve books about children and movie violence as well as *every* book in the library about TV whether or not it has anything to do with children and violence.

Problems with Keyword Searching

Although keyword searching offers solutions to some of the problems inherent in subject searching, it does have disadvantages of its own. The first problem is a lack of comprehensiveness. Keyword searching does not necessarily retrieve every record on a subject. The only way to get a comprehensive list of material is by identifying the proper subject heading. For example, if you look up **Y2K bug** as a keyword phrase, you'll find only the records that contain this phrase. These records will all list **Year 2000 date conversion** as a subject heading. Not every book with this subject heading, however, will contain the keywords **Y2K bug**, since that's really a slang form of the subject. If you return to traditional subject searching and look up **Year 2000 date conversion** (which is often as easy as just clicking on the subject heading within the book record you have found), you will get a complete list of all the books on this topic.

Another drawback is the retrieval of irrelevant material. Keyword searching often retrieves irrelevant material because it takes words out of context. If you wanted a book about the architecture of Boston and were to enter **boston and architecture**, in addition to retrieving all the records for books about Boston architecture, you would also retrieve all the books about architecture that were published in Boston but not necessarily about Boston. Remember that basic keyword searching generally picks up words throughout the record including the publisher field.

Finally, keyword searching often retrieves peripheral material. Because keyword searching searches throughout the item record that might also include chapter titles, notes, summaries, and so on, you might also get a lot of books that contain only a small amount of information on your topic.

Field-Specific Searching

To lessen the effects of the second two problems just mentioned, you can limit your keyword searches to particular fields in a record. Web-based catalogs have certainly simplified this advanced level of searching. For example, for books about Boston architecture, you could indicate that you want these words located only within the subject headings of records and/or within the titles. Often this choice is made by selecting it from a pull-down menu on an advanced search page, but your catalog might employ another method.

Limiting keyword searches to subjects and titles is an excellent way to refine your search if you find that you have retrieved too many records or irrelevant records. *Field-specific searching*, as this technique is called, is also useful when searching electronic periodical indexes, as well as when using Web search engines and many other computerized databases that we will be discussing farther along in this book.

Now that you know the ins and outs of using an online catalog, take it for a spin and find some books on your topic. The best way to remember the techniques I explain in this book is to actually use them in real-life situations. You would never have learned how to drive a car unless you got behind the wheel at some point, started the engine, and hit the road, no matter how much you had read the driver's manual.

Three

Read the Map: Library Organization

New York City is commonly referred to as "The Big Apple." I was curious to find out why, so I did a little research. I found so many different explanations for the nickname that I became a bit frustrated. Even though I never found a definitive origin for the "Apple," it is certainly easy to understand why it's called "Big" after a brief visit; in fact, this almost seems like an understatement.

Finding your way through the streets of Manhattan, the main borough of New York City, might initially appear to be confusing if you are unfamiliar with the city, but despite its immensity, it's not that hard to get around. Whoever originally designed the road system laid out most of the streets in a gridlike pattern. So instead of all the streets being uniquely named, most were simply numbered. This makes it possible through a little trial and error to determine if you're going in the right direction even if you've never been there before.

I realized how logically New York City is arranged one day during Christmas break my freshman year. I took a bus into New York City by myself for the first time ever and had planned to meet some friends at Fifth Avenue and 34th Street—the famous end point of Macy's Thanksgiving Day Parade. The bus stopped at the Port Authority terminal at Eighth Avenue and 42nd Street. Alone and a little anxious in a big city, I was hesitant to ask for directions. So I just started walking down Eighth Avenue and the next block happened to be 43rd Street, so I knew I was going in the wrong direction. I turned around. When I reached 34th Street, I took a left because that just felt like the direction to go. My gut feeling was correct, but I could have simply turned around if it was not. When I came to Seventh Avenue, I breathed a sigh of relief. Going two blocks farther, I reached my destination.

Libraries can be compared, in a way, to Manhattan. Although usually much quieter, libraries can be big and often overwhelming. When people go into them, they often think it will be hard to find their way around. Libraries these days certainly contain much more than just books, but books still take up the most space, and books are often what you look for when you begin your research. The average college library contains hundreds of thousands of books; a large university library contains millions! But you can easily find what you need amid this overwhelming amount of material if you understand how everything is organized. With this understanding, you will also be able to locate periodicals, videos, and other nonbook material in the many libraries that organize these collections in the same way as their book collections. There is even a Web directory, *CyberDewey* (*www.anthus.com/CyberDewey/CyberDewey.html*), that arranges its listings using the same system that has been in use for over a century to arrange books in public libraries and some small college libraries.

THE LAY OF THE LAND

There really weren't too many libraries before the nineteenth century, except for those catering to the needs of academic institutions or individuals who could afford to pay dues. Each one of these private libraries organized its books in a different way. But in the 1800s, several factors—all related to the Industrial Revolution—led to the rise of libraries. A more technologically literate society was needed to support the rise of industry, so public education and literacy became widespread. At the same time, technological advances in printing, which transformed it from a manual to a mechanical process, made the production of books less expensive and easier. Finally, Andrew Carnegie and other leaders of industry donated large sums of money to support the building of new libraries. With more books, more people reading them, and more libraries, there was a greater need for a standard system of organization. Two systems actually emerged: the Dewey Decimal Classification used in many public libraries and some smaller college libraries; and the Library of Congress (LC) Classification, the standard in larger public institutions and most academic libraries.

In order to get your hands on the books you have identified in the online catalog, you need to be familiar with either the Library of Congress system or, less frequently, Dewey Decimals, depending on which is used by your library. Students constantly ask for help because they can't find a book (which is fine; librarians are there to help); but in many cases this is simply because they don't understand the system that is used to arrange them. There are probably countless other students who don't ask for directions, but instead just wander through the stacks wasting precious time and getting frustrated. To avoid getting lost in the stacks, here's a crash course in what is called *classification*.

Every book in a library is given a unique number—a *call number*—to indicate its location. You find out a book's call number by looking it up in the library's online catalog. With Dewey Decimals as well as the LC Classification, the subject matter and the author's name determine the number a book is given, which in turn determines its location on the shelf.

Table 3.1 Dewey Decimal Classification.

000–099   **General works**—like encyclopedias, but a lot of other topics have been thrown in over the years ranging from Bigfoot and UFOs to computers and the Internet.

100–199   **Philosophy**—this also includes psychology, astrology, witchcraft, and related topics.

200–299   **Religion**—200–289 includes Christianity, while all other world religions are crammed into the 290–299 section.

300–399   **Social science**—includes sociology, political science, economics, and related topics.

400–499   **Languages**—here you will find books about individual languages as well as linguistics in general.

500–599   **Natural sciences** (as opposed to applied sciences, which are covered in the next section)— books on mathematics, astronomy, chemistry, physics, and life sciences are found here.

600–699   **Technology**—includes applied sciences ranging from medicine and engineering to cooking.

700–799   **Fine arts**—includes painting, sculpture, music, performing arts, television, games, and the like.

800–899   **Literature**—includes classic literary works as well as literary criticism, but does not usually include contemporary fiction and other works not considered "classic" (these are generally kept in a separate fiction section arranged by author).

900–999   **History**—in addition to historical topics, includes biographies which are often kept in the 920 section.

The Dewey Decimal Classification

The Dewey Decimal Classification divides knowledge into ten broad categories from 000 through the 900s. Each broad category is subdivided into ten more sections, which are each further subdivided into ten smaller sections, and so on until you get down to the level of individual books that have call numbers involving decimals. For example, if you are interested in literature, the books you want are located between 800 and 899. More specifically, books of American literature are between 810 and 819. This is further subdivided into sections such as poetry, drama, and essays, each designated by a whole number. Nineteenth-century American writers are primarily found within the 818 section. Although individual libraries may differ slightly in the exact call numbers they assign to their books, a copy of Henry David Thoreau's classic *Walden* might have the specific call number 818.3. To summarize this sample hierarchical scheme:

800–899 Literature
  810–819 American literature
    818 Nineteenth-century American literature
     818.3 Thoreau's *Walden*

The part of the number following the decimal point can be a bit confusing. Just to review some basic math (you didn't think library research was going to involve math, huh?), decimals don't have the same value as whole numbers. For instance, *Walden*, as well as books about *Walden*, at 818.3 will actually be found after a book with a number like 818.298, because .3 is more than .298. When using decimals, zeros get dropped, so .3 is really the same as .30 or .300, and so on to infinity. When zeroes are appended, it's easier to see that .300 is greater than .298.

The Dewey Decimal Classification has some inherent weaknesses. Its hierarchical scheme has a strong bias toward Western culture as well as a lack of concern for what we refer to as "political correctness." A similar situation is obvious with the emphasis on American, British, and Western European literature. The literature of countries that were considered alien to most people in nineteenth-century America—Asian, African, and Middle Eastern countries as well as Russia, Poland, and many others—is squeezed between 890 and 899.

Another problem with this system is that, as new subjects arise, they must be shoehorned in somewhere; the original nineteenth-century scheme had no place for topics such as computer programming and television. Computer books are commonly thrown in with the encyclopedias, and you'll usually find the books about television along with all the books on movies in the fine arts section, specifically 791.4 (not even a whole number!). Because of this, books in these and other unforeseen areas must have long and complicated call numbers in order to give each a unique location.

The Library of Congress Classification

The Library of Congress Classification is more complex. It is used by some larger public libraries, many academic libraries, and, of course, by the Library of Congress, which designed it in the nineteenth century to organize the increasing number of books in its collection. This national library has grown from a small, one-room, legal collection established in the Capitol in 1802 for the use of Congress to a massive institution that contains over one hundred million items. Such a vast collection requires a more specific scheme of organization; Dewey Decimals are not sufficient for the task.

The LC Classification breaks all of knowledge into 20 broad categories indicated by letters of the alphabet (see Table 3.2). You'll find encyclopedias in the A section, atlases in the G section, and literature in the P section. You may think it's odd that Military and Naval Science are considered top-level categories, but you have to remember that the

Table 3.2 Library of Congress Classification.

A **General works** such as encyclopedias.

B **Philosophy**, **religion**, and **psychology**.

C **History**—special topics like archaeology, genealogy, and general biography.

D **World history**.

E/F **American** and **Canadian history**.

G **Geography** (mostly)—in addition to atlases and books about various geographic areas, you'll also find books about the environment, dancing, and sports.

H **Social sciences**—includes sociology, economics, and business.

J **Political sciences**.

K **Law**.

L **Education**.

M **Music**.

N **Fine arts**—includes painting, sculpture, and architecture.

P **Literature**—also includes theater, movies, and television.

Q **Natural sciences**—mathematics, astronomy, chemistry, physics, life sciences, and so on.

R **Medicine**.

S **Agriculture**.

T **Technology**—other applied sciences like engineering, photography, and cooking.

U **Military science**.

V **Naval science**.

Z **Bibliography**—library science as well as bibliographies that list materials on various subjects.

original purpose of the scheme was to serve the needs of the government. The basic categories are subdivided alphabetically. For example, while books on literature are given the letter P, English literature is PR and American is PS.

The LC system is alphanumeric. Following the initial one, two, or, occasionally three-letter code are numbers that further divide a particular topic. If you're looking for humor (which you may be needing if you've gotten this far in the chapter), go to the PN6160s. Jerry Seinfeld's book *Sein Language* usually has the call number PN6162 .S358. How would you go about getting your hands on this item? Locating the book on the shelf is akin to locating Fifth Avenue and 34th Street in Manhattan, since the books are all shelved in a certain order. But the Library of Congress system is more complicated than this analogy implies because, like the Dewey Decimal Classification, it also uses decimal points as well as an often confusing jumble of letters and numbers. It's more like getting to Macy's, finding the shoe department, and selecting a pair of shoes in your size.

So you want to get a copy of *Sein Language* at PN6162 .S358. Here are the steps to take:

- First, you have to find out where the P section is located. Consult a floor chart or ask your friendly librarian.
- Once you find the general P Section, finding the PNs is simply a matter of alphabetical order—they'll be between the PMs and the POs.
- When you find the PNs, follow the call numbers numerically until you get to 6162. Don't confuse this with the Dewey system and look for 616.2. If you try looking for PN616.2, you'll wind up in a totally different section from PN6162 and see lots of books about classical, medieval, and renaissance literature—certainly not what you had in mind.
- Once you have found PN6162, switch back to the alphabet to find S (which stands for the author's last name).

- After finding the S section, you encounter the trickiest part of the LC Classification: the dreaded decimals. You need to look for .358 (just drop the S now that you've found it). Recalling our discussion of decimals earlier in the chapter, would *Sein Language* at PN6162 .S358 be found before or after a book called *You Have a Hang-up If . . .*, which has been assigned the call number PN6162 .S37? Is .358 greater than .37? No, because .37 is the same as .370, which is obviously greater than .358. What about a book called *Copycat* at PN6162 .S2513? If you've got a grip on decimals now, you'll have no problem determining that *Copycat* will be found before *Sein Language*. To make sure this is all clear, let me list the order in which you'd find the books:

PN6162 .S2513 *Copycat*
PN6162 .S358   *Sein Language*
PN6162 .S37   *You Have a Hang-up If...*

At first glance, you might have thought these books would actually go in the opposite order, but if you just insert some mental zeros, it becomes clear that this is the proper arrangement.

The year of publication is often included at the end of the call number, but I have omitted it here so the numbers appear a bit less daunting. This date is important only in distinguishing one edition of a book from another.

I admit I've gotten into some picky details here. In reality, what often happens is this: You find the general section you need such as PN6162 and then, realizing that the books in this section are arranged by author's last name, simply scan the titles on the shelf to find what you need, rather than strain your eyes looking at those little call numbers on the book spines. This can work effectively in many situations.

Library of Congress call numbers, however, are not always as simple as in the humor section. I mentioned before that when classification systems were developed in the nineteenth century, many subjects did not even exist. So when books about such topics as airplanes, television, and extreme sports were written, they had to be fit in somewhere. As a result, a lot of books have been crammed into very small call number ranges and therefore must have very long call numbers with lots of digits, letters, and decimals.

For example, let's take a look at the section of the library that contains books about the Internet. Although a decade ago you would have found few books about the Internet in most libraries, now there are thousands, and all of them are usually designated by call numbers starting with TK5105.875 .I57. A particular book like *The Complete Idiot's Pocket Reference to the Internet* has the lengthy call number TK5105.875 .I57 G65. If you break down this call number, it's really not too much harder to find than *Sein Language*; it just looks more intimidating.

- After finding TK and 5105, you look for .875 the way you look for any decimal.
- Then you find .I57 by first locating the Is and then .57.
- Finally, after finding G (which stands for Goldman, the author's last name), you regard 65 as a decimal also, even though there's no decimal point before the G. In the LC scheme, any number after the initial whole number is regarded as a decimal. So *The Internet for Windows* by David C. Gardner at TK5105.875 .I57 G368 will be found before TK5105.875 .I57 G65.

There is another confusing aspect of the LC Classification. Where's the fiction section? Libraries that use LC numbers usually don't have a separate fiction section as do public libraries using Dewey Decimals. This is because the LC scheme is intended more for research than for recreational purposes. Fiction is most often put in the literature section (designated by call numbers beginning with P), side by side with criticism of the various works. The same is true for biographical material; whereas Dewey libraries tend to put most biographies in the 920s, LC libraries have them scattered throughout the collection depending on the occupation of the person about whom the book is written.

Many books are hard to classify because they might involve more than one subject. A book about the psychology of women, for example, may be classified in the HQ section rather than BF, which is the primary psychology section, because HQ contains books on women's studies. Depending on how you look at the book, it could fit in either section. If this book on the psychology of women was of a more medical nature, it could even be placed in the RCs. If there's only one copy of the book, however, it can have only one distinct call number, so the librarian who catalogs the book must make a choice. This same problem can occur when a book is classified with the Dewey Decimal system. This is why it is important to use the online catalog rather than just meander through the stacks; you may find that books on basically the same subject are in different call number areas.

Once you get familiar with the system used to organize books, however, you can do some "educated browsing." Although, in Chapter 1, I said that browsing is not an effective way to do research, if you practice "educated browsing" in certain call number areas, you often serendipitously find some useful material. Of course, if you're looking for something really narrow, you may have problems. Restrict your browsing to more general information on a topic. To be an "educated browser," look up your subject in the online catalog and find a few relevant books and their call numbers. Then, after locating these books in the stacks, take a look at what other books are on the shelf nearby.

As a side note, another way to find further material once you're in the stacks and have found a few books is to look in the back of each of these books for a bibliography of sources. If you notice any titles in the bibliography that look pertinent, look them up in the online catalog to see if your library has them.

I mentioned that both the Library of Congress and Dewey

Decimal classifications were developed as indirect responses to the Industrial Revolution. As we undergo another period of change, the Information Revolution, these two systems still serve to give some order to what could easily be chaos. I mentioned earlier that there are some Web directories that organize material based on these schemes. For example, *CyberDewey* is a site that categorizes many other sites using the Dewey scheme. The designer of this directory, David A. Mundie (who is not a librarian), explains why these traditional classification systems still deserve our attention: "It became clear that library classifications were ideally suited to my organizational needs. They have evolved over a long period of time to solve exactly the sorts of problems that confronted me, and they embody a tremendous amount of collective wisdom."[1]

---

1. David A. Mundie, "Organizing Computer Resources," *CyberDewey*, 1995. <www.anthus.com/CyberDewey/Organizing_computers.html> (11/5/02).

Four

Stop for Directions: Reference Sources

I magine getting lost while driving through a desert. It's the hottest time of the day, and the road ahead of you stretches on for miles; you're not even sure if you're going in the right direction or if you should have gone left at that last fork in the road. You're running low on fuel, you can't find a map in the glove compartment, and, to top it off, you're getting thirsty! It's been fifty miles since you passed a gas station and you have no idea how long it will be before you come to another.

This situation is what comes to mind when I think of students who must complete those library "scavenger hunts" that require them to answer a series of trivial questions using reference sources. The professor's intention is good—to have students learn how to use the library's resources, especially those in the reference room—but the result is usually a frustrated student who can't wait to leave the library. You shouldn't be sent to the library to complete such an assignment or any research project without some clear directions. That's what this chapter will give you.

Reference sources enable you to find quick answers to your questions as well as broad information on paper topics to either get you started with your research or check a fact before handing in your final draft. They are the basic necessities of research, just as water and fuel are indispensable when driving through the desert. In this chapter, I'll introduce you to the major categories of reference sources by posing some trivial yet interesting questions and then showing you how to find the answers effectively. If you encounter a similar sort of question in the future, you'll know where to go. This chapter will not inundate you with lists of book titles accompanied by dull descriptions. Instead, I will highlight the types of sources that I consider among the most helpful and give you a few examples.

The reference room, however, can no longer be considered just a physical place in the library building, because many reference books are now available online or on CD-ROM, and more are becoming available all the time through services like netLibrary. Most libraries provide access to some computerized reference sources through their Web sites. Despite the difference in format between print and computer versions, however, the content remains similar in the emerging virtual reference room.

We'll be discussing the evaluation of Web sites later on, but a few words are appropriate here. If something is available for free, it's usually of a lower quality or includes a lot of advertising. For example, online encyclopedias like *Britannica* and *Encarta* allow you to access some information for free, but only after you have had to view a number of advertisements, and they do not provide you with complete entries unless you are a paying subscriber. Libraries must subscribe to most of the good computerized resources I will discuss just as you subscribe to cable TV to get commercial-free programming. If your library's Web site provides links to Web-based reference sources, these sources have probably been selected because of their quality.

So be a bit cautious when using the Web for reference sources. And be extremely skeptical if you feel the urge to simply use a Web search engine to find the answer to your question—you will probably retrieve a lot of irrelevant junk and even inaccurate information (but more about that later).

No college library will have every source mentioned here, but a good library will have a large percentage of them, as

well as many other titles that fall into the general categories of reference material described in this chapter.

ENCYCLOPEDIAS: A GOOD STARTING POINT

Q: How much did the *Titanic* weigh?
A: The *Titanic* weighed 46,328 tons, or over 92 million
   pounds! (I still don't understand how such a heavy thing
   could float, but that's a research question for another day.)
   SOURCE: *Encyclopedia Americana*, 1994 International
   ed., s.v. "Titanic."

Encyclopedias, whether computerized or in their traditional place upon the bookshelves, are often a good place
to start your research because they provide concise, factual
overviews on a vast number of subjects. Encyclopedias are
probably one of the first things that come to mind when you
hear the term "reference books." You will usually find the
volumes of general encyclopedias in the A call number section of the reference room if your library uses the LC Classification or in the 030s if Dewey is used, along with other
general works.

The most scholarly and in-depth encyclopedia is the
Encyclopaedia Britannica. Here are others you are likely to
find:

- *Encyclopedia Americana*—This is suitable for college
  level research.
- *Academic American Encyclopedia*—This is also a good
  starting point for your research projects.
- *Collier's Encyclopedia*—Written on a high-school level,
  this encyclopedia is intended for a more general audience.
- *World Book Encyclopedia*—This should be a last resort
  because it is not intended for college-level research.

Many encyclopedias are now available online. The Web

version of the *Encyclopaedia Britannica* can be found at *www.britannica.com*. After a barrage of pop-up ads, you can read the first paragraph of the Titanic entry, but the full text will not be available to you unless you are a paying subscriber. There is also Microsoft's *Encarta Online* encyclopedia (*encarta.msn.com/encnet/refpages/artcenter.aspx*), which has no print equivalent. Using *Encarta*, you can find the weight of the Titanic, as well as information on thousands of other common topics, but you also have to look at an annoying amount of advertising.

The Importance of Consulting the Index

Often, the most important part of an encyclopedia or any reference source or book is its index. Without it you may never find what you need. Many electronic reference sources also use a computerized version of a back-of-book index. These are not indexes in the traditional sense. You might think that since databases are searchable by keywords an index would be unnecessary, but users are starting to realize that they can wander just as aimlessly through a Web site as through a book, so site designers are incorporating indexes into their products to serve the same purpose. Instead of looking up your subject and turning to a certain page in a book, however, you click on your subject and go to a particular page within a site.

The following question demonstrates the importance of book indexes:

Q: Who were the Plastic People of the Universe?

A: No, they weren't Saturday morning TV cartoon characters. This was the name of a Czechoslovakian band whose members were arrested in the mid-1970s along with other intellectuals, artists, and students who belonged to the Charter 77 movement for Czech independence, which protested the repressive measures imposed after the Soviet invasion. The band's arrest motivated the playwright Vaclav Havel and others to sign a manifesto demanding respect for human and civil rights. SOURCE: *Encyclopedia Americana*, 1994 International ed., s.v. "Czechoslovakia."

The answer is in the C volume of *Encyclopedia Americana*, not the P volume. If your subject is not in the appropriate lettered volume, it's probably not broad enough to have its own entry in a general encyclopedia. Look it up in the index, which is the last volume of the set. If you look up Plastic People of the Universe in the index, you are directed to volume eight (the C volume) under the heading "Czechoslovakia."

The index is also handy because you can locate all the entries relating to your topic, not just the one that starts with a particular first letter. For instance, if you look up "deserts" in the index volume of *Encyclopedia Americana*, you'll be referred to a number of subtopics in different volumes that all relate to the main topic, such as specific places (Death Valley and the Mojave Desert) and related topics (cactus, oasis, and the infamous dust devil—a mini-tornado filled with sand). This will give you more information than would be contained in the D volume alone. It's similar to the online catalog providing you with cross references for books.

Indexes are the key to using most reference sources and are also helpful in finding information in many nonfiction books in the circulating collection. If you're having trouble finding the information you need in a particular source, chances are there is an alphabetical index either in the back of a one-volume source or in the final volume of a multivolume set (like a general encyclopedia) that will indicate on which page to locate your information.

Subject-Specific Encyclopedias: Off the Main Drag

Q: How did the mood ring, that short-lived jewelry fad of the 1970s, really work? And why did Sophia Loren's mood ring make tabloid headlines in 1975?

A: Inside the stone of the mood ring were heat-sensitive liquid crystals derived through a chemical process from sheep's wool, the same stuff that had been used for years in hospital thermometers. In 1975, Sophia Loren stopped a press conference because to her horror her mood ring had turned black—a very bad omen, indeed! SOURCE: Jane and Michael Stern, *The Encyclopedia of Bad Taste*, (New York: HarperCollins, 1990), 218.

I couldn't find any entries for mood rings in traditional general encyclopedias, and I checked four different ones. This is where subject-specific encyclopedias sometimes come in handy. The subjects covered by the *Encyclopedia of Bad Taste* include a variety of fads of the 1970s such as mood rings, disco, and bell bottoms (which have experienced a recent revival) as well as the short-lived phenomena of other decades.

Whereas each major general encyclopedia consists of many volumes, specialized encyclopedias are often just one volume, although some are multivolume sets. Besides finding topics that may not be covered in general encyclopedias, these specialized books can go into much greater depth. More common specialized encyclopedias include the *Encyclopedia of Philosophy*, the *Encyclopedia of Religion*, and the *Encyclopedia of Popular Music*. Think of any major subject area and there's probably an encyclopedia that focuses on it.

There are also encyclopedias that focus on narrower subjects. In addition to the *Encyclopedia of Bad Taste* cited above, you might also find such offbeat titles as the *Star Trek Encyclopedia* and the *Encyclopedia of Unbelief*. How do you locate these helpful sources? I'll reiterate a technique that we've discussed before that will come in handy here—keyword searching. For example, if you want to find out if there is an encyclopedia about sleep in your library, enter the keyword search **encyclopedias and sleep** in the online catalog. This works well when looking for any subject-specific reference source. If you need a timeline of women's issues, try a search for **chronologies and women**; if you need a film term defined, search for **dictionaries and motion pictures**.

Sometimes encyclopedias have confusing titles that use the word *dictionary* instead of *encyclopedia*. For example, the *Dictionary of American History* is a multivolume work that I wouldn't describe as a dictionary because of its length and depth of coverage. Ordinarily, the basic difference between an encyclopedia and a dictionary is in the length of the entries: A dictionary implies brief definitions, while an encyclopedia contains lengthier essays. The line between these two types of sources sometimes gets a little blurry.

DICTIONARIES: WHAT DO YOU MEAN?

Q: What are the following: 1) phrenophobia, 2) soogee-moogie, 3) the best boy?

A:

1) Phrenophobia is a "morbid fear of having to think, endemic to politicians, or a morbid fear of losing one's mind" (common also to many college students).
2) Soogie-moogee is a slang term for a "mixture containing soda used for cleaning paintwork and woodwork on boats" (not to be confused with sudzy-dudzy or squeegie-weegie).
3) If you've ever sat through the closing credits of a movie, you've probably wondered what the best boy does. Basically, he or she is the chief assistant to the chief electrician (or gaffer) on a motion picture set.

SOURCES:

1) Stuart Sutherland, *The International Dictionary of Psychology* (New York: Continuum, 1989), 325.
2) John Ayto and John Simpson, *The Oxford Dictionary of Modern Slang* (Oxford: Oxford University Press, 1992), 232.

3) Ira Konigsberg, *The Complete Film Dictionary* (New York: New American Library, 1987), 27.

Aside from the usual language dictionaries you consult from time to time, like *American Heritage* or *Webster's*, there are numerous specialized dictionaries such as those used above. As mentioned before, it's sometimes hard to draw the line between encyclopedias and dictionaries, but you could also consider these as mini-encyclopedias providing brief definitions of terms used in a particular field of study in an alphabetical format. There are many dictionaries available on the Web. Many are listed at the Ramapo Catskill Library System's site "DeskRef: Sources for Quick Answers" (*www.rcls.org/deskref*), a really great site that also provides links to a wide variety of free, but surprisingly useful, online reference sources from encyclopedias and dictionaries to shoe-size conversion charts and used car price guides.

ATLASES: BEYOND WHERE

Q: What were the five largest American cities in 1790? in 1870?

A: Philadelphia was actually the largest city in 1790, followed by New York and then Boston, Charleston, and Baltimore. New York had overtaken Philadelphia by 1870; Brooklyn (which is today considered part of New York City) was third, followed by the more westerly cities of St. Louis and Chicago.
SOURCE: Kenneth T. Jackson, ed., *Atlas of American History* (New York: Scribner's, 1984), 97, 177.

Atlases are commonly used to find out where a place is, how to get to it, what its geographic features are, and so on. This is handy for many research purposes and most students are familiar with the straightforward atlases that are basically books containing maps of physical places. But atlases come in other varieties also. The question above reveals the usefulness of atlases that provide historical information. There are also atlases that focus on certain themes such as the *Atlas of the Supernatural*. Although the maps are usually supplemented with more text than a general atlas, at the heart of these books are the maps that relate geography to a particular subject.

STATISTICAL SOURCES: HOW MUCH? HOW MANY?

Q: How many pounds of mozzarella cheese did the average American consume in 1999? Was this an increase over previous years?

A: In 1999, the average American ate 9.2 pounds of mozzarella. This was a substantial increase; in 1990, the amount was 6.9 pounds, and in 1980, only 3 pounds. Are we eating more pizza, perhaps? I couldn't find that out in this source, but I'm sure this fact is somewhere. SOURCE: *Statistical Abstract of the United States* (Washington, D.C.: U.S. Government Printing Office, 2002), 129.

Statistical Abstract of the United States is a good place to check for any sort of national statistical information. It is an annual collection of statistics derived from the government census as well as from private sources. When you locate the appropriate table, be sure to note the year of the information given. Just because you're using the most recent volume doesn't mean you're getting current information. *Statistical Abstract* is also available online at *www.census. gov/statab/www*.

Q: What percentage of U.S. households have at least one television set? How about in Angola?

A: Of all U.S. households, 98 percent own at least one television (34 percent have two; 40 percent have three or

more); in Angola, there are 48 TVs for every thousand people—a rate of 4.8 percent.
SOURCE: *World Almanac and Book of Facts* (Mahwah, N.J.: Funk and Wagnalls, 1998), 188, 762.

If you require statistics for another country, a good place to check is the *World Almanac and Book of Facts*. Although this source includes primarily U.S. information, there is a long section that contains a brief entry for each country.

Other helpful sources for more in-depth international information:

- *Statesman's Yearbook*
- *Country Studies* (also available at *lcweb2.loc.gov/frd/cs*)
- *CIA World Factbook* (also available at *www.odci.gov/cia/publications/factbook*)

The U.S. government is an excellent provider of statistical information and most of it is now available online. In addition to *Statistical Abstracts* and the sources listed above, you can find a wide range of reliable sources at *www.fedstats.gov*. Government sources are also good because they are free. I don't include too many Web site addresses in this book because most of the reliable reference sources are fee-based and your library may not subscribe. But government sources are available to anyone with Web access.

CHRONOLOGICAL SOURCES: WHEN?

Q: When was the first successful circumnavigation of the earth in a balloon? How long did it take, and who accomplished this milestone?

A: On March 20, 1999, Dr. Betrand Piccard of Switzerland and Brian Jones of Britain went around the world in 19 days, 1 hour, and 49 minutes (much less than "80 days"), becoming the first balloonists to successfully circle the earth.

SOURCE: "Round-the-World Balloon Flight Succeeds," *Facts On File World News Digest*, 25 March 1999: 199.

Facts On File World News Digest is a news service that provides biweekly summaries of world events. It's an excellent source for not only finding out when something happened, but also who did it and other key information. In the print version, the digests are collected in a binder throughout the year and then bound up into annual volumes. Your library might also subscribe to *Facts On File* on the Web.

Q: In what years did the following motion picture "firsts" occur:

1) sound movie
2) Academy Awards
3) drive-in theater
4) psycho-slasher film?

A:

1) 1927 (*The Jazz Singer* with Al Jolson)
2) 1929 (not a very suspenseful event since all the winners were announced in advance)
3) 1933 (in New Jersey)
4) 1978 (*Halloween*)
   SOURCE: Bruce Wetterau, *New York Public Library Book of Chronologies* (New York: Prentice Hall, 1990), 552–557.

For events of a more historic or thematic nature spanning a number of years, such as motion picture history, chronological reference sources are very helpful. There are numerous books covering different historical topics or themes, such as American wars (*Chronology of World War II*) or women's history (*Chronology of Women's History*). Try the keyword search method in the online catalog to find these sources (for example: **chronology and world war ii** or **timeline and world war ii**). There is also an excellent book called *Timetables of History* that, for any given year, will indicate what was going on simultaneously in politics, art, society, and more.

BIOGRAPHICAL SOURCES: WHO ARE YOU?

Q: What occupations did Martha Stewart pursue before gaining fame and fortune as the famous domestic maven?

A: Not surprisingly, Martha was employed as a professional caterer, but she also worked as a model and a stockbroker. What a multitalented dynamo!
Source: "Martha Kostyra Stewart," *The Complete Marquis Who's Who*, 2001, available from *Biography Resource Center* [online database] (Farmington Hills, Mich.: The Gale Group), <http://www.galenet.com/servlet/BioRC> (20 November 2002).

I used the online version of *Who's Who*, called *The Complete Marquis Who's Who*, available from an online database called *Biography Resource Center* produced by InfoTrac. It includes such *Who's Who* sources as *Who Was Who in America* (for famous deceased people), *Who's Who in Entertainment*, and *Who's Who of American Women*, which are also available in print. These sources provide brief entries on notable people. There is usually contact information of some sort (not in *Who Was Who*, obviously) and all of the important dates and accomplishments in the person's life.

Q: How did Picabo Street, who won a gold medal in skiing at the 1998 Winter Olympics, get her unusual first name?

A: Her parents, true flower children of the 1960s, had intended for their daughter to choose her own name when she was old enough. When they applied for passports, however, they were informed that "Baby Girl" was not acceptable as a name, so they chose a place name meaning "shining waters" in the language of the Sho-Ban Indians of Idaho. Their daughter loved playing peekaboo and, although not a Native American, was a third generation Idahoan, so it seemed like an appropriate name to them.

SOURCE: *Current Biography Yearbook* (New York: H. W. Wilson, 1998), 556–559.

If you want more in-depth information on a notable person, one place to turn is *Current Biography*. This series provides biographical essays on people who made an impact on the world in a particular year in some field—perhaps politics, sports, or entertainment. It is available both online and in print.

There are many other sources for biographical information in the typical reference collection, some of which may focus on a particular country, ethnic group, time period, or occupation. There are a few I consider worthy of special mention because I find myself directing students to them time after time. The *Dictionary of American Biography* covers figures of note in American history. *The Scribner Encyclopedia of American Lives* is a bit more contemporary, providing essays on famous individuals who have died since 1985. Since biographical information on writers is always in such high demand, *Contemporary Authors*, which provides biographical sketches on current writers, and its companion series *Dictionary of Literary Biography*, which contains lengthier essays on writers living and dead, are highly used.

DIRECTORIES: GETTING IN TOUCH

Q: Who is the director of the Society of Earthbound Extraterrestrials, and how can I contact him?
A: The director's name is Otamer Tllak. But unlike E.T., don't "phone home;" contact him at the headquarters of the society at (780) 444–8367 (that's 444–UFOS), or e-mail him at see@alien.org.
SOURCE: *Encyclopedia of Associations*, 38th ed. (Detroit: Gale Research, 2002), 1:793.

Real people are great sources of information. Let's say you're doing a research paper on UFOs and you want to interview someone to add pizzazz to your paper. Or maybe you just want to be sent some literature in the mail on a particular organization or find out the address of its Web site. To identify organizations, learn their missions, and find out how to get in touch with them, use the *Encyclopedia of Associations* (also available online or on CD-ROM). This is not an encyclopedia in the true sense; it is more accurately defined as a directory, since it directs you to something.

Other useful directories:

- *Who's Who in America*: We've already looked at this series as a source of biographical information, but it is also a directory since it often provides contact information.
- *United States Government Manual*: It provides contact information for governmental agencies and officials (also available at *www.access.gpo.gov/nara/nara001. html*).

QUOTATION SOURCES: SAY WHAT?

Q: Who said the following:

1) "The most beautiful thing we can experience is the mysterious. It is the source of all true art and science."
2) "I learned three important things in college—to use a library, to memorize quickly and visually, and to drop asleep at any time given a horizontal surface and fifteen minutes. What I could not learn was to think creatively on schedule."

A:

1) You may know this man by his more famous quote, "E=mc2"—Albert Einstein.
2) Agnes de Mille, the famous choreographer, in her book *Dance to the Piper*.

SOURCE:

1) *Bartlett's Familiar Quotations*, 14th ed. (Boston: Little, Brown, 1968), 950.
2) *The New York Public Library Book of 20th Century American Quotations* (New York: Warner Books, 1992), 165.

Books of quotations serve three purposes:

• to find quotes pertaining to a particular theme
• to find some quotes attributed to a particular person
• and, conversely, to find out who said a particular quote

There are two basic varieties of quotation books: thematically arranged and chronologically arranged. The best known book of quotations is *Bartlett's Familiar Quotations*, which belongs to the latter type although you can also find quotes on specific themes by looking up keywords in the index.

The source for the quotation from Agnes de Mille is a thematically arranged quotation book. Such compilations are great for finding a quote to use on a specific subject but not so useful in identifying the source of a quote.

BIBLIOGRAPHIES: WHERE DO I GO FROM HERE?

Q: What books were written about the Beatles between their rise to stardom in the early 1960s and their disbandment at the end of that decade?

A: Over 30 books were written, including such memorable works as *The Beatles: A Study in Drugs, Sex, and Revolution*, which contended that these four lads from Liverpool were really part of a communist plot to take over the world, and *Up the Beatles Family Tree*, a genealogical study of the Fab Four.

SOURCE: Roman Iwaschkin, *Popular Music: A Reference Guide* (New York: Garland, 1986), 226–232.

　　Although you might think of a bibliography simply as the list of sources at the end of a book or as the list you must compile for your own research paper, there are also a wide variety of book-length bibliographies to be found in the typical reference room. These books can be enormously helpful because they are focused on one particular subject and provide citations for books, periodical articles, audiovisual material, and rare unpublished works relating to the subject.

　　As you can see, the reference room, whether real or virtual, is an oasis where your thirst for information can certainly be quenched. I have only scratched the surface in this chapter. The reference librarians at your library can assist you in using the sources I have mentioned and can suggest other resources that might be helpful in your research.

Five

Find Your Way: Periodicals and Periodical Indexes

You certainly shouldn't head out on a long road trip without a map, especially if you're concerned about arriving at your destination on time or without getting lost. The purpose of maps is to show you the way—to guide you on your journey. Similarly, you shouldn't begin your search for periodical articles without first consulting a periodical index. These indexes, as I'll detail in this chapter, are like road maps for finding your way through periodicals, helping you to determine which issues will contain articles on your topic. Wandering around the periodical room and browsing through issues of magazines and journals is a highly ineffective way to search for articles. You will certainly feel lost if you proceed in this manner. And if you believe that Web search engines will lead you to the sources you need, think again; articles from published sources are not commonly available on the Web for free. The most efficient way to find articles is to use periodical indexes.

As I emphasized in Chapter 1, the first step on the road of research is defining your topic. So before you go about searching indexes for articles, it's a good idea to have your subject chosen. It's okay to have a broad topic, but, as you proceed with your research, you will have to hone in on a specific idea to pursue.

TYPES OF PERIODICALS

The next thing you have to decide is what type of articles you need. Although one thing all periodicals have in common is that they are published on an ongoing basis (daily, weekly, monthly, quarterly), there are different varieties of periodicals: scholarly journals, trade journals, general magazines, newspapers, and so on. Before proceeding further, let me explain some of the important differences between types of periodicals since they, along with your topic, will determine which indexes you search.

The terms *journal* and *magazine* are often used synonymously. When your professors instruct you to find journal articles, however, they usually don't have *People, Time,* or *Cosmopolitan* in mind. Professors generally want their students to use scholarly journals in their research; these are periodicals containing articles written by experts in particular fields of study, frequently individuals affiliated with academic institutions. Scholarly journals tend to be very specialized in their subject focus and are research oriented, containing examples of primary literature sources. Primary sources are those in which scholars who have conducted research report their findings (as opposed to secondary sources, which report on someone else's activities). Another characteristic of academic journal articles is that they are often "peer reviewed." This means that before an article is accepted for publication, it must be deemed worthy by a group of the author's colleagues. Academic journal articles usually have bibliographies at the end citing all the sources referred to in the text; this can be helpful, leading you to a variety of sources that may aid in your research. There is another type of journal that is useful to those doing business research—the trade journal. Trade journals are periodicals written for people working in a specific industry.

The term *magazine*, on the other hand, brings to mind general-interest publications that you would find on any newsstand. Magazines are intended for a general audience and don't go into as much technical depth as scholarly journals. They may be easier and more enjoyable to read, but they are usually not as valuable for your own research. If you pick up a copy of *People*, you might see articles such as "The 50 Most Beautiful People," and "Ben Affleck: Sexiest Man Alive." Were you to look at the table of contents of an issue of the *Journal of Popular Culture*, however, you'd see articles like "Staking Her Claim: Buffy the Vampire Slayer as Transgressive Woman Warrior" and "The Evolution of the Seven Deadly Sins: From God to the Simpsons." The difference in content reflected in these titles is pretty obvious. The physical difference is also apparent. Magazines tend to be glossy publications with eye-catching covers, while journals are often more dull looking—but, just as you should not "judge a book by its cover," don't overlook a periodical simply because of its appearance.

INDEXES: YOUR ROAD MAPS FOR FINDING ARTICLES

In Chapter 4, I pointed out that the index in the back of a book is an important tool. Instead of browsing through the entire book looking for what you need, you simply turn to the alphabetically arranged index in the back of the book and look up your subject to determine what page to turn to. Many Web sites are also beginning to provide "site indexes," which link you to the page you want within a site. Periodical indexes do the same sort of thing by referring you to articles in specific issues of various periodicals. There are many different indexes, each one focusing on periodicals in a particular subject area.

Most often today, you will go to a computer to use an index. These electronic indexes will provide not only references to articles, but often the text of the articles themselves. In the past, students had to rely on print indexes to find articles. Unlike the card catalog for books, which can be considered obsolete, print indexes still serve a purpose, as I'll explain later.

A Basic Example of an Electronic Index

The following is a simple example of how you would find articles using an electronic index. It uses InfoTrac's *Expanded Academic ASAP*, a popular periodical index in libraries today. Most online indexes have a similar structure. The next chapter describes some of the other common electronic databases you are likely to find in a college library and will highlight a wide variety of other indexes you might use. Chapter 7 will go into greater detail on how to search computerized databases, including indexes. For now, I just want to give you a general idea of how you go about finding articles.

Suppose you needed to find articles about Mount Everest. If your library subscribes to InfoTrac, it is probably just a click away on the library homepage. InfoTrac is a service that provides a collection of indexes each focusing on a different subject. By selecting *Expanded Academic ASAP*, which covers hundreds of academic journals as well as popular magazines, the opening search screen will be displayed as shown in Figure 5.1.

In the search box you enter the subject **Mount Everest** and click "search." As a result, the screen shown in Figure 5.2 appears, which displays a list of subject headings for this topic.

It starts by listing the heading you're looking for; this is followed by all the other headings starting with **Mount Everest**. Underneath each heading you can click on the word "View" in order to see the citations for the articles pertaining to that heading. The main heading for Mount Everest also has the option to "Narrow by subdivision." This basically provides you with subheadings you can search individually; I will explain this further in a moment. For now, clicking "View" brings up a screen containing a list of citations, as displayed in Figure 5.3.

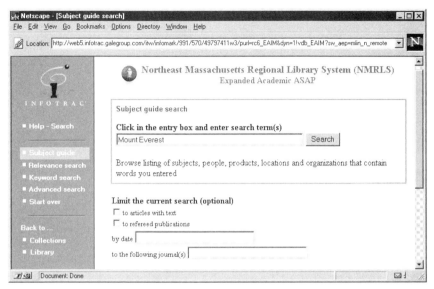

Figure 5.1: Opening search screen for InfoTrac's
Expanded Academic ASAP.

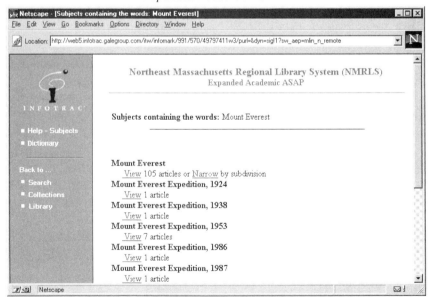

Figure 5.2: Subject listing for **Mount Everest** in InfoTrac's *Expanded
Academic ASAP*.

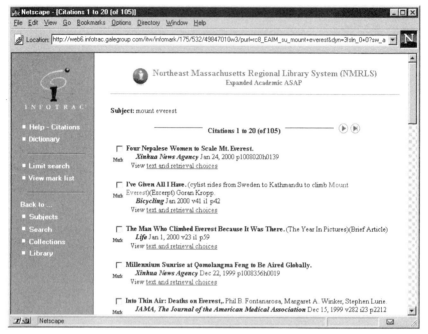

Figure 5.3: List of citations under the subject **Mount Everest** in
InfoTrac's *Expanded Academic ASAP*.

The citations are listed in groups of 20 in descending
chronological order—that is, most recent first. A citation is
a reference to an article that provides all the information you
need to locate that article.

The third article is "The Man Who Climbed Everest Because It Was There," which appeared in the January 2000
issue of *Life*. No author is cited. The citation goes on to give
you the volume and issue numbers—in this case: volume 23,
issue one. The volume number generally corresponds to the
year of publication. *Life*, which recently ceased publication,
had been published as a monthly magazine for 23 years as
of January 2000. This is the first issue of the year. The article starts on page 59.

Below the citation is a link to view the text. Just click here
to see the complete text of the article. Although for this par-

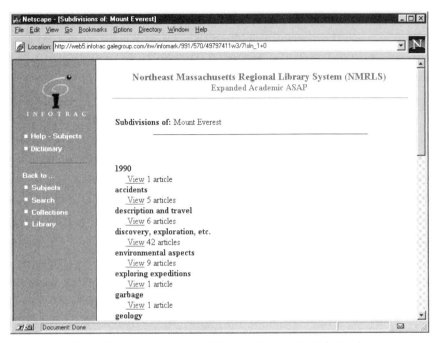

Figure 5.4: Subdivisions of **Mount Everest** in InfoTrac's *Expanded Academic ASAP*.

ticular topic the first few articles are available, this index, like many others, does not always provide the complete text. We just got lucky. Often, just the citation is available, especially for older articles. Since these may still be excellent sources, check to see if your library subscribes to the periodical cited. You don't have to limit yourself to the articles that are available online.

This search was rather broad and found over 100 articles. If you wanted a smaller and more relevant list of articles, you could click on the option to "Narrow by subdivision" as displayed in Figure 5.2. The subdivisions of **Mount Everest** are shown in Figure 5.4.

Each subheading has a smaller number of articles. You can view one article about Mount Everest in 1990, five articles about accidents on the mountain, six describing the place and travel, a larger group of forty-two that focus on discovery and exploration, and so on.

Just as most electronic indexes have a structure similar to InfoTrac *Expanded Academic ASAP*, you may also recognize similarities to the structure of online catalogs discussed in Chapter 2. As with online catalogs, you will often see cross references to aid you in your subject searching. This example was an easy search focusing on a concrete topic. Things are not always so simple. For this reason, electronic indexes have more advanced capabilities involving keyword searching and limiting, which I will discuss in Chapter 7. In the end, however, what you get is a list of citations, some of which will provide you with the text of the articles.

Print Indexes

Despite the prevalence of electronic indexes, I consider it important to understand how traditional print indexes are used for three reasons:

- Some indexes still have no computerized equivalents, although this is becoming increasingly rare.
- It's always good to have a reliable backup if the computers go down in your library or if it's so busy at the end of the semester that you can't get time on a computer.
- The most important reason—if you want to find articles published before 1980, you will often need to use a print index. You may also need to use print indexes for articles published during the 1980s. Although there is some retrospective coverage, most electronic indexes cover only periodicals dating from the early 1990s (when online indexes emerged into widespread usage) to the present.

What if you wanted to find articles written about the first successful climb to the top of Mount Everest in 1953 by Sir Edmund Hillary? You specifically want articles written at

---

EVEREST, Mount

Assault on Everest. Newsweek 41:86 My 25 '53

By camera to the top. il Newsweek 43:54 Ja 25 '54

Commando tactics challenge Everest. G. Soule, il Pop Sci 162:105-7
My '53

Conquest of Everest. Time 62:24-6 Jl 6 '53

Conquest of Everest. il Life 34:18-25 Je 29 '53

Conquest of Everest, by J. Hunt. Review America 90:540 F 20 '54. P.
Temple

    Commentary 18:343-8 O '54. S. Marcus; Reply with rejoinder. J.
    Hunt. 18:475 N '54

    New Repub 130:"17 F 1 '54. B. Bliven

Earth's third pole, Everest. M. Herzog. il N Y Times Mag p 12-13+ My
31 '53

Everest at last. Life 34:48 Je 15 '53

Figure 5.5: Listing of citations under the heading **EVEREST, Mount**
in *Reader's Guide to Periodical Literature*.

that time, not articles written more recently about that event.
So electronic indexes that focus on the 1990s forward would
be useless. Instead, go to a print index. *Reader's Guide to
Periodical Literature* in book form was once *the* place to
search for articles in popular magazines. Volumes of
Reader's Guide go all the way back to 1900. It is now available in electronic form but shares the growing market with
such online services as InfoTrac and EBSCO*host*.

A print index like *Reader's Guide* consists of individual
volumes that correspond to each year of periodicals covered.
So, finding the volume for the time period you are interested
in, look up **Mount Everest** in the alphabetically arranged
Reader's Guide. You are referred to **EVEREST, Mount**.
Under that heading you will see a listing of articles as displayed in figure 5.5.

As you can see from these citations, *Reader's Guide* covers only the most popular periodicals such as *Newsweek*,
Popular Science, *Time*, *Life*, and so on. The information

given in these citations is basically the same as you would find in any electronic index except that the citations are a bit more abbreviated. The first article, "Assault on Everest," appeared in *Newsweek* (volume 41, issue number 86) on May 25, 1953. The second article, "By Camera to the Top," includes pictures (that's what the abbreviation **il** indicates).

Reader's Guide often includes cross references just as in an online catalog. Under many subject headings you will come across *see* and *see also* notations. These are helpful since the difficult aspect of using a print index, especially when looking up a more complex topic, is finding the proper subject heading. The search for Mount Everest is deceptively easy; you will often find that your subject cannot be defined by a single heading and that you must skim through many irrelevant articles under a broad heading in order to find the specific one you need. Once again, this is why electronic indexes are such an improvement over the print versions.

Index Selection

There is a wide variety of indexes focusing on particular fields of interest. The next chapter will introduce you to many of them. Just as you don't usually rely on a world atlas when taking a short trip, but instead use a road map of the specific area of the country you're traveling in, you don't use *Expanded Academic ASAP* or *Reader's Guide* for every topic. Since many topics are interdisciplinary in nature, you can certainly find articles in more than one index.

For example, if you were doing a paper about the geology of Mount Everest, you might also want to consult a resource like *General Science Index*. To find articles about the tourism industry in Nepal and the growing interest in commercial expeditions to the summit of Mount Everest, you could take a look in a business index like InfoTrac's *Business ASAP*. *Biography Reference Bank* would provide citations to material about famous climbers of the world's highest mountain. You could also use a newspaper index like the *New York Times Index* to find newspaper articles.

When selecting which index to use, first become familiar with which ones are available at your library. Then consider the following:

- What is the subject focus of the index? Choose an index that pertains to the subject area for your topic. As the previous example demonstrates, you don't have to limit yourself to one single index.
- What type of material does it cover? Scholarly journals, trade journals, general magazines, newspapers, or a mixture? Your decision to use or not use a particular index will depend on your needs.
- What years are indexed? Be aware of what general time period is covered by the index. As explained before, you wouldn't want to search an electronic index that includes citations only for journal articles published in the 1990s if what you really want are articles published in the 1950s.

GETTING YOUR HANDS ON THE ARTICLES

So once you know where to go, how do you actually get there? In other words, once you have citations, how do you get your hands on the articles? If you've used an electronic index, you may have been able to retrieve the full text online. Still, electronic indexes provide many citations without the text. Don't pass these by just because you have to do some extra work. If you've used a print index, you'll definitely have to track down the articles. Since every library is arranged a bit differently, the paths will be somewhat varied, but I'll try to give you a general idea of how to arrive at your destination in the sometimes confusing land of periodicals.

Formats

You will find articles in three basic formats: hard copy, microfilm, and electronic. While hard copies are the actual physical magazines, newspapers, or journals, microfilm provides a space-saving copy on film that can be read and reproduced by using a microfilm machine. Believe it or not, at one time, microfilm was considered the latest in information technology, since a whole month's worth of newspapers or a year's worth of magazine issues could fit on one roll of film. Today, microfilm seems outdated, awkward, and simply a pain to use. Still, it is common in many libraries and will be around for some time to come. Technically, *microfilm* is a type of *microform*; the other is *microfiche*, which comes in the form of cards.

Many libraries now subscribe to individual journals in electronic format through such services as Project Muse and EBSCO*host*'s Electronic Journal Service (EJS). Electronic indexes often provide text right on the screen, and sometimes graphics too. Increasingly, you can even view an exact replica of the article that, when printed out, looks like a high-quality photocopy of the actual article. In addition to printing out the article, most online indexes enable you to e-mail the article to yourself or to download it to a disc. These two options help to save money and paper.

Generally, full-text electronic sources are recent in their focus. But a number of databases are emerging that do have an historical focus. Accessible Archives provides access to the full text of numerous publications from the eighteenth and nineteenth centuries through such databases as *The Civil War: A Newspaper Perspective*, *Godey's Lady's Book*, and *American County Histories to 1900*. *ProQuest Historical Newspapers* is a database that provides the digitized full images of every page of *The New York Times* and *The Wall Street Journal* back to their beginnings in the nineteenth century. Other newspapers will be added to this database, including *The Washington Post* and *The Christian Science Monitor*.

Although some periodicals have their own Web sites that might provide selected articles for free from current issues and maybe even selected ones from older issues, to access the full "archives" you usually have to be a subscriber. And searching through these individual Web sites can be just as inefficient as browsing through hard copy issues of periodicals.

You may be tempted to use only those articles that are readily available online so you can avoid using microfilm or having to track down the hard copy in the periodical room. By disregarding any index citations that might send you to the microfilm or periodical room, however, you may miss out on the most helpful information for your paper. You should not pick a periodical source based on its format, but rather on its content. In the end, you'll be better off because having better sources makes it easier to write your research paper.

Periodical Organization

While the nonelectronic copies of older magazines and newspapers are generally stored on microfilm, past issues of scholarly journals are often in book form, a year's worth of issues bound into a single volume. Not all libraries organize their periodicals in the same way. In some libraries, periodicals (both hard copy and microfilm) are arranged alphabetically by title. In other libraries, each periodical is assigned a call number depending on its subject focus. All the same rules of Library of Congress or Dewey Decimal call numbers then apply. Bound volumes of journals arranged by call number may be shelved in the periodical room or in the same stacks where circulating books are found. Your library may even have closed stacks so you must request the material and don't have to worry about how it is arranged. Familiarize yourself with the method of organization used to arrange periodicals in your library. Don't hesitate to ask a librarian for help if you can't easily determine the organizational scheme yourself.

What If Your Library Doesn't Have It?

There are tens of thousands of magazines and journals being published in the world today, along with thousands of newspapers. With so many periodicals available, a single library can't subscribe to every one, so academic libraries generally subscribe to what are known as the core (or most important) journals in those fields in which the college specializes. They may also get some of the peripheral (or less essential) journals in these same fields as well as many general magazines, major newspapers like *The New York Times*, and the local papers for the area in which the library is located. Your library should have some sort of a list of all its subscriptions either in paper form or on its Web site. You may also be able to search for a periodical title in the same way you look for a book title in the online catalog.

If your library doesn't subscribe to the periodical you need to complete your paper or have it available in electronic format, don't lose hope. If you have allotted yourself sufficient time for obstacles along the way (as I advised you to do in the beginning of this book), you can take advantage of the resources of other libraries.

A librarian can help you determine whether a periodical is in another library in your area. If the library is part of a consortium, there may be a list of the holdings of the other member libraries available. You can then either go to the library yourself to copy the article (since most periodicals don't circulate) or you may even be able to have a copy sent to your own library.

If the periodical cannot be located in the immediate vicinity, your library can obtain it through interlibrary loan (ILL). Even if the article you need is in an obscure scholarly journal held by only a handful of libraries in the country, your library's ILL department can request this article and usually get it to you within a week or two. The time factor involved here is the main drawback of ILL and the reason that many students, starting their papers too late, cannot take advantage of this valuable service.

Finding articles is an essential part of your research. For some narrow or very recent topics, as I mentioned previously, articles may provide you with the only information you can find. So don't get lost and frustrated. Keep going in the right direction by using the appropriate periodical indexes.

Six

Choose the Vehicle:
Selecting Electronic Resources

Just as there are many makes and models of cars and the decision about which one to buy is often a difficult one, the range of electronic resources available in your library or through your library's Web site is sometimes overwhelming. How do you know which databases to use? Fortunately, you don't have to pick just one, and you also don't have to spend any money to search them. But you can sure waste a lot of time if you use an inappropriate resource; you may never even find the information you need. This chapter will make sense of the ever expanding variety of electronic databases and give you the background you need to feel comfortable selecting the right ones. It will focus on the content of computerized resources, enabling you to choose wisely, while the next chapter will focus on using these resources, building upon the fundamentals of how to search an online catalog discussed in Chapter 2.

TYPES OF ACCESS

There are two main ways of accessing electronic resources: on CD-ROM, which is becoming less prevalent, and online, usually through the Web. CD-ROMs are discs that can store a huge amount of data in the form of text as well as graphics, animation, and video. An entire encyclopedia can fit on a single disc; so can a periodical index containing citations for an entire decade of articles. If you search the disc properly, you can quickly find any piece of information stored on it. In general, CD-ROMs can only be used within the library. Many CD-ROM databases have been replaced by online versions, but you still find this format in just about all libraries because some databases are still available only on CD-ROM, and CD-ROM versions can be cheaper than the equivalent online database. Another advantage of CD-ROMs is that they can often work more quickly than an online database—you don't get caught in the "heavy traffic" caused by many people being on the computer network at the same time. But CD-ROMs have limitations; even with their seemingly large storage capacity, databases—especially those that provide the full text of articles—are becoming too large to fit on a single disc. It's also harder to update a CD-ROM. Online databases tend to have more recent information because they can be updated at a central location often on a daily basis, while an updated CD-ROM has to be produced and then sent to a library to be installed (usually monthly or quarterly).

The other means by which you gain access to electronic databases is online. Today, this generally means via the World Wide Web. Access is usually restricted to these Web databases. Sometimes you can use them only within the library, or you may be able to get to them from the library's homepage in your dorm room or at any computer on campus. Another way of restricting access is to implement passwords (often your student ID number) so you can use the resources from virtually any location on or off campus.

Both online and CD-ROM resources share many advantages over traditional resources in print. Since multiple volumes of an index, an encyclopedia, or some other type of reference source can be stored in a single database, you save all the time it would take you to repeat your search in each volume of a print source. Computerized indexes also take up a lot less physical space than books, so it is possible to include abstracts for each citation. Another advantage is that you don't have to copy citations by hand or make poor quality photocopies; instead, you can print out any pertinent information you find; you can also download to a disc, and, in some cases, e-mail records to yourself. It's also much easier to search a computerized resource because you can use keywords.

The cost and quality of the online databases I will highlight in this chapter differentiate them from the free Web resources I will discuss in Chapter 8. In other words, when you search a Web-based periodical index or reference source, you are generally using a resource that has undergone a rigorous editorial process that enhances its quality and accuracy. Your library pays for the database and access is limited. There are exceptions, however. For example, governmental Web sites are excellent sources of authoritative information and many are now freely accessible on the Web. There are also some sites, like Ingenta, that provide free access to the indexing of articles but charge a fee for the full text.

Usually, if a database is available for free on the Web, it is because the producer accepts advertising. For example, while searching for information about the *Titanic* on the *Britannica* Web site, which provides free access to the full text of seventy periodicals, I clicked on the link "Magazines" and got a list of article titles. Clicking on a title brought up the full text absolutely free. My excitement was somewhat short-lived, however, when I reviewed the results. There certainly were quite a few articles, and some of them from scholarly journals, but it seemed that many of the articles were quite irrelevant including quite a number from *Football Digest* about the Tennessee Titans, and *Science News* about Saturn's moon Titan. While searching through the list, I was also treated to a number of pop-up ads encouraging me to join the Army, as well as continuous ads in the margin of the Web page advertising *Britannica*'s products. Considering that the relevant articles could have been found through services available on the Web sites of practically any college library, it hardly seemed worth the effort of closing all the pop-up ad boxes or printing out a copy full of marginal ads.

TYPES OF DATABASES

There are four main types of electronic databases used in libraries:

- Bibliographic—These are indexes providing citations to articles and perhaps abstracts but no complete text.
- Full-text—These databases include indexes that provide the text of articles, and reference sources, such as encyclopedias, and other electronic books that include the complete textual content of the print version.
- Full-image—These databases provide an exact replica of the print version; for instance, InfoTrac's *Expanded Academic ASAP* is partially a full-image database because it includes copies of some articles that, when printed, look even better than photocopied versions of the same articles from the hard copies of the periodicals.
- Multimedia—These resources combine text and graphics with animation, video and sound. For example, *Grolier's Multimedia Encyclopedia* contains all 21 volumes of the text of *Academic American Encyclopedia* as well as pictures, maps, animation, video, and sound. You can look up "John Kennedy," for instance, and, in addition to reading about him, watch video clips from his most famous speeches.

Sometimes these types overlap in a single resource. A database may provide bibliographic citations for some articles, full text for others, and complete images for others.

POPULAR ELECTRONIC RESOURCES

For the next few pages, I will describe in greater detail the most popular online services in libraries and the databases they provide. As with the reference sources I described in Chapter 4, not every library will have every one, but you should be able to access at least a few; if not, you might want to consult another library in your area. Before proceeding, it is important to understand that an online service usually provides access to a number of different subject-specific databases. InfoTrac, for example, is not one particular database, but the name of a service that includes a variety of resources. Think of an online service as a car dealership; the individual databases provided are like the different car models. If you go to a Toyota dealer, you don't ask to see a Toyota; instead, you probably have specific models in mind, like a Corolla, Tercel, or Camry. In the same way, when you use InfoTrac or one of the other online services, you need to select a specific database to search. The majority of databases available are periodical indexes, but there is also a wide variety of online reference sources.

Among different databases and database providers there is often overlap in what information is covered. An index like InfoTrac's *Expanded Academic ASAP*, for example, covers many of the same periodicals as EBSCO*host*'s *Academic Search Elite*, but there are certain titles that are unique to each of these databases. To offer another metaphor, it's like shopping in a mall. Similar types of stores will carry a lot of the same merchandise. But, if one store doesn't have exactly what you want, you simply go to another. The bottom line is that there is no single source to consult when researching your topic. You may have to go through a process of trial and error and search more than one database. It's okay to search multiple databases; what you want to avoid is wasting your time searching a database that is inappropriate.

You will also find that some of the same databases are

available through different online services. For example, an index to educational materials called *ERIC*, which is produced by the United States government, is accessible though EBSCO*host*, SilverPlatter, and FirstSearch. Online services don't have to actually produce the databases included in their collections, although some do. Two online services that will be highlighted in this chapter, SilverPlatter and Ovid, produce no original material at all, but provide access to hundreds of resources produced by other companies. The purpose shared by all online services we will look at is to provide access to databases, and each has its own unique interface for searching the database.

I don't want to get too bogged down in details like how many periodicals each database indexes, how much full-text coverage is provided, or what years are included. I started to do this and realized that all the descriptions began to sound the same: "hundreds (maybe thousands) of periodicals indexed, text available for a large percentage, and coverage generally for the past ten years or so." Besides, these descriptions are constantly changing and you won't remember them anyway. Instead, I want to give you a sense of the subject focus of each source since that's what matters most when deciding which ones to use.

InfoTrac

Gale Group produces InfoTrac databases. *Expanded Academic ASAP*, which we saw in the last chapter, is part of the InfoTrac collection of resources. Although some of the Infotrac databases are also available on CD-ROM, the common way of accessing them is through InfoTrac Web which indexes more titles and provides more full-text coverage. *Expanded Academic ASAP* is a popular resource in academic libraries because it covers a wide selection of scholarly journals.

Other InfoTrac databases you are likely to encounter include:

- *General Reference Center* and *InfoTrac OneFile* — These indexes focus on more popular general interest publications.
- *Biography Resource Center* — This database indexes biographical material and provides the full text from a variety of reference sources published by Gale as well as numerous periodicals. *Contemporary Authors* is one of the popular reference sources included in *Biography Resource Center*; this resource, which provides biographical sketches for just about any writer you can think of who is currently living or who died after 1960, is also available as a separate stand-alone database.
- *Business and Company Resource Center*, *General BusinessFile ASAP*, and *PROMT* — All these sources index business magazines and trade journals.
- *Health and Wellness Resource Center* and *Health Reference Center* — These indexes cover medical and general health topics.

Simply stated, if your library has InfoTrac, it is one of the best places to start with your research, and in general, *Expanded Academic ASAP* is the most appropriate database to use for finding academic material.

EBSCO*host*

EBSCO*host* is similar to InfoTrac. This service provides access to a number of resources including the *Academic Search* databases, which are similar *to Expanded Academic ASAP* in content, covering a wide variety of subject areas. Your library might subscribe to the *Elite* or *Premier* editions, which differ only in the number of full-text titles provided. Among the other indexes that EBSCO*host* produces are:

- *MasterFILE* — This database for popular magazines is more common in public libraries.
- *Business Source* — This covers business magazines, trade and academic journals.

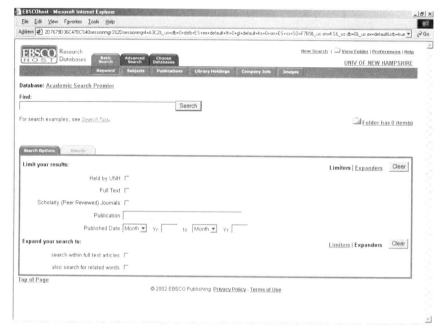

Figure 6.1: Opening search screen for
EBSCO*host*'s *Academic Search Premier*.

- *Newspaper Source*—Besides indexing articles in leading national newspapers like *The New York Times*, *The
  Wall Street Journal*, *USA Today*, and *The Christian Science Monitor*, the text of over a hundred local, regional,
  and international papers is included as well as
  newswires such as the Associated Press.

In addition to the indexes that it produces, EBSCO*host*
also provides access to many resources produced by other
companies. Your library will probably not subscribe to all
of these, but you might see such reference sources as *Co-
lumbia Granger's World of Poetry* and *Wilson Biographies
Illustrated*, and such indexes as *ERIC* and *Medline*.

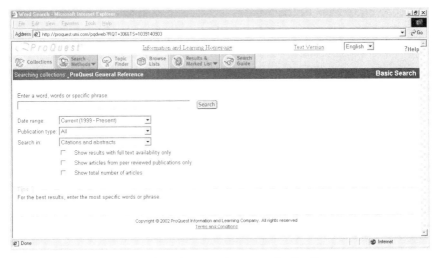

Figure 6.2: Opening search screen for ProQuest.

ProQuest

ProQuest databases were among the first to provide not just the full text but also the page images for periodicals covered by many of its indexes. Access to ProQuest databases is provided through the ProQuest service itself as well as through FirstSearch, which will be described further along. Similarly, the ProQuest service provides access not only to its own databases, but to many published by other companies. Among the popular ProQuest databases are:

- *Periodical Abstracts* and *ProQuest General Periodicals*—Both of these indexes provide broad coverage of popular as well as academic periodicals. While *Periodical Abstracts*, as its title implies, is primarily an index that provides abstracts, *ProQuest General Periodicals* provides the full images of the articles indexed.
- *ProQuest Newspaper Abstracts*—This resource indexes and abstracts the leading national and regional newspapers including *The New York Times* and *The Wall Street Journal*. Your library might also subscribe to the

separate ProQuest databases that provide the complete text of several major newspapers. *ProQuest Historical Newspapers*, mentioned in the previous chapter, goes back to the nineteenth century in its coverage.

- *ProQuest Business Periodicals* and *ABI/INFORM*— These indexes provide abstracts for business and management journals including many international journals.

H.W. Wilson

The most well-known Wilson index is *Reader's Guide to Periodical Literature*, which has been available in print since 1900. The H.W. Wilson Company has published subject-specific indexes in print for many years, and all of these are now available in electronic versions. All of the indexes are available in *Abstract* and *Full Text* editions. Wilson has its own online service, WilsonWeb, but also makes its databases available through EBSCO*host*, FirstSearch, and SilverPlatter. Wilson indexes are subject-specific as indicated by the titles below.

- *Applied Science & Technology Index*—covers subjects relating to practical applications of science including engineering, computers, telecommunications, transportation, and waste management.
- *Art Index*—coverage of fine arts.
- *Biography Reference Bank*—combines all of the information and indexing contained in all Wilson sources relating to biography. This includes *Biography Index*, which covers both periodicals and books about famous people, as well as biographical reference sources like *Current Biography* and *World Authors 800 BC to Present*. Your library might instead subscribe to *Wilson Biographies Plus*, which provides the full text of all the biographical reference books that Wilson publishes but not the indexes.

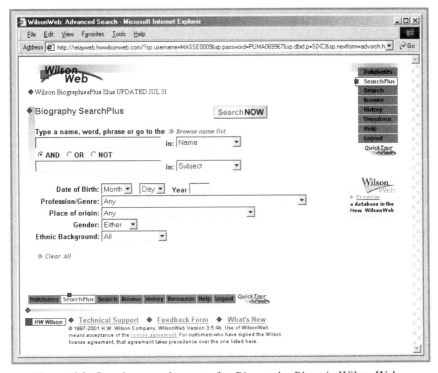

Figure 6.3: Opening search screen for *Biography Plus* via WilsonWeb.

- *Book Review Digest*—includes excerpts from book reviews in popular review sources.
- *Business Periodicals Index* (also available as *Wilson Business Full Text* and *Wilson Business Abstracts*)—covers general business magazines and trade journals.
- *Education Index*—as the title implies, covers topics relating to education.
- *General Science Index*—covers articles on pure science (as opposed to applied science).
- *Humanities Index*—covers a variety of subjects including literature and language, history, philosophy, archaeology, classics, performing arts, history, and religion.
- *Reader's Guide to Periodical Literature*—the "classic"

index; most libraries subscribe to either *Reader's Guide Abstracts* or *Full Text*. *Reader's Guide Retrospective* provides indexing for periodicals published all the way back to 1890.

- *Social Sciences Index*—coverage includes such topics as anthropology, area studies, economics, political science, psychiatry, psychology, social work and public welfare, sociology, urban studies, women's studies, and so on.

Wilson also produces the *OmniFile* databases, which basically combine the education, general science, humanities, and social sciences indexes along with *Wilson Business Full Text* and *Reader's Guide Full Text*.

FirstSearch

FirstSearch, produced by an organization called OCLC (Online Computer Library Center), is primarily a service that provides access to the databases of other publishers. It currently gives library users access to more than 70 resources. This collection includes many of the Wilson and ProQuest databases and other popular indexes such as *ERIC* and *Medline*. Many reference sources are also provided, such as the *World Book Encyclopedia* and *Facts On File World News Digest*. All of these databases can be easily searched using the FirstSearch interface.

Although the majority of databases included in FirstSearch are produced by other companies, OCLC does produce a popular database called *WorldCat*, which is like an online catalog for the world. With one search you can search online catalogs worldwide. More practically, if a book is not at your library, you can easily find out if it is at another library in your area without searching numerous catalogs. This database provides information not only on books, but also on a wide variety of nonbook material, including Web sites. OCLC has incorporated a database previously

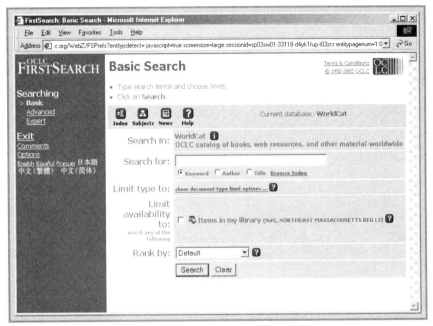

Figure 6.4: Opening search screen for OCLC's FirstSearch.

known as *NetFirst* into *WorldCat*. Now you can enter a subject or keyword search and, by limiting your search to
Internet files, retrieve a list of links to relevant sites. In this
way, *WorldCat* serves as a very efficient search engine that
retrieves highly relevant material. Because the sites included
are assigned Library of Congress subject headings and are
evaluated for quality, this database can be much more useful than the free Web search engines that retrieve a large pro-
portion of irrelevant and low quality resources.

LexisNexis™ *Academic*

Always popular in newsrooms and corporate libraries,
LexisNexis™ used to be a rare find in academic libraries
except for large research institutions. But the *Academic* service is specifically geared toward the college market. The

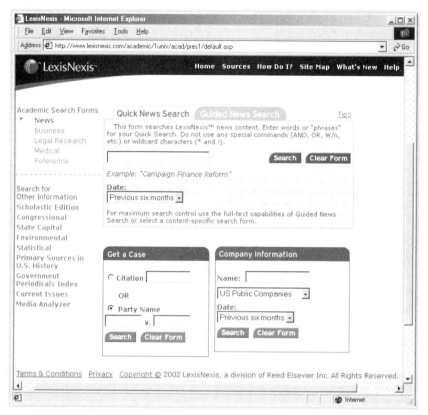

Figure 6.5: Opening search screen for LexisNexis™ *Academic*.

emphasis of LexisNexis™ is on current information regarding news, business, legal, and medical topics, rather than on scholarly research. It provides access to the full text of thousands of sources, including newspapers and magazines, world news services, newswire services, television transcripts, SEC filings, and federal and state laws and regulations. Many sources are updated daily.

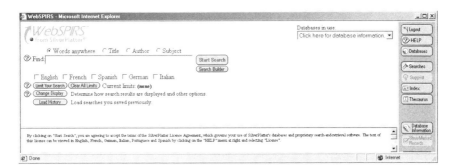

Figure 6.6: Opening search screen for SilverPlatter's *MLA Bibliography*.

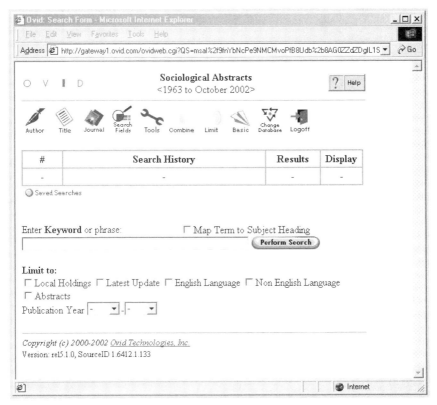

Figure 6.7: Opening search screen for Ovid's *Sociological Abstracts*.

SilverPlatter and Ovid

Neither SilverPlatter Information nor Ovid Technologies produce any of their own content, but they provide access to many databases produced by other companies. SilverPlatter's collection of over 250 databases and Ovid's collection of over 90 include those of companies like H.W. Wilson and ProQuest. Among the more popular databases provided to libraries by both Ovid and SilverPlatter are *PsycINFO*, *ERIC*, and *Medline*. SilverPlatter also provides access to such reference sources as *Who's Who* and *Peterson's College Guides*. Each service has some highly technical databases that you probably won't need to use for typical college research papers.

SilverPlatter and Ovid, which are actually two companies now owned by the same parent company, each have a unique interface for searching the databases on both CD-ROM and online. SilverPlatter databases can be searched using the SilverPlatter Information Retrieval System (SPIRS). WebSPIRS is the software used when searching on the Web and WinSPIRS and MacSPIRS when using Microsoft Windows or MacIntosh. Ovid databases can be searched on the Web via Ovid Online or on CD-ROM using Ovid Windows.

Dialog@CARL

Dialog is an online database service that has been around for a long time but has been available to students for only a few years. Since this extensive collection of highly specialized databases was very complicated and expensive to use, you usually had to have a librarian search it for you. Dialog was available only as a service for professionals in corporate and academic libraries rather than for library users. But the Dialog@CARL version of this service, which is produced by The Library Corporation, can be thought of as "Dialog Lite." As a select group of about 300 Dialog databases accessible in a Web-based format, Dialog@CARL is user-

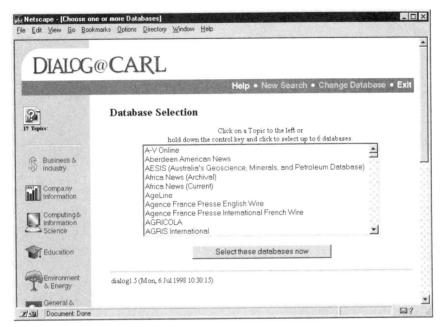

Figure 6.8: Homepage for Dialog@CARL.

friendly enough for anyone to search. Since Dialog@CARL provides so many databases, it subdivides them into 17 subject areas. In addition to areas relating to law, medicine, and business, Dialog has such categories as Humanities and Arts, Sciences, and Technology and Engineering. There is overlap among these subjects because some Dialog databases fit into more than one category.

Dialog@CARL probably won't be your first stop—it's more like the "end of the road." Many of the databases are very specific; for instance, the full text of individual newspapers not found elsewhere, like the *Anchorage Daily News* and the *South China Morning Post*, reference resources such as the *American Library Directory*, and extremely narrow indexes such as *World Surface Coatings Abstracts* (which probably won't help you much with your Freshman Comp paper). If your library provides access to Dialog@CARL and

Figure 6.9: An example of an "eBook" available via netLibrary.

you haven't found what you need using the other online services available, see what it has to offer.

NetLibrary

NetLibrary provides access to electronic versions of over 40,000 print books. These "eBooks" include a variety of current popular works, scholarly titles, and older public domain materials. An individual library picks the eBooks that it wants in its customized collection and then students can "check out" these titles to read online. Once an eBook is checked out, it cannot be read by another library user until it is "returned." You can't print out the whole eBook, so you do have to read most of it on the screen. You can bookmark pages and do something you would NEVER do with a regular library book—write notes. These notes are saved in your personal account to be viewed by you again if you check out the same title. Another nice feature is the ability to search the text of the book for a term, which is similar to looking up a subject in the index in the back of a regular book.

"Free" Web Sites Worthy of Mention

So far, all of the resources I have listed will be available to you only if your library subscribes to them. Because they are not free databases, they are generally of a higher quality than most of the free resources you will find on the Web. "You get what you pay for," as they say. There are a few resources, however, available to anyone with access to the Web that fall into the scope of this chapter. One such category is governmental information. The other includes Web sites that index periodicals for free but charge a fee for the full text.

United States Government Databases

The United States Government is one of the most prolific publishers in the world. Some of the popular databases already mentioned in this chapter are compiled by governmental agencies. For example, *Medline* is the National Library of Medicine's database to more than eleven million articles published in over four thousand medical journals. Although it is one of the resources available via EBSCO*host*, FirstSearch, and SilverPlatter, and other services, you can also access it for free by going to *www.nlm.nih.gov*.

ERIC is another database offered by various online services that can also be accessed at a governmental Web site. *ERIC*, which stands for Educational Resources Information Center, is supported by the U.S. Department of Education and the Information Institute of Syracuse University and provides access to abstracts of over one million documents and journal articles concerning educational topics. It is available at *askeric.org/Eric*.

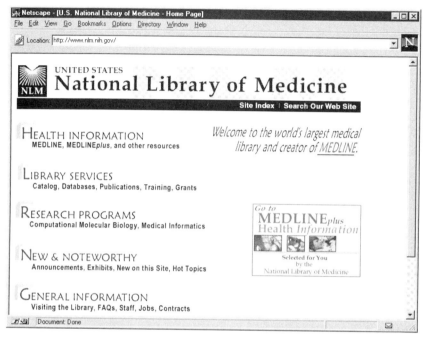

Figure 6.10: The National Library of Medicine's
homepage providing free access to *Medline*.

Another important resource is the *GPO Monthly Catalog*,
also known as the *Catalog of United States Government
Publications*, which indexes the publications of the Government Printing Office. While some of the publications indexed are available online, all can be obtained at any one
of the numerous Federal Depository libraries throughout the
country. To use this catalog, go to the GPO Access Database
List at *www.access.gpo.gov/su_docs/databases.html*, where
you will also find a list of other governmental databases
available, ranging from the complete *Budget of the United
States Government* to the *Weekly Compilation of Presiden-
tial Documents*.

You may be wondering why your library would provide
access to these databases through subscription-based services
if they're available for free. When a database is available

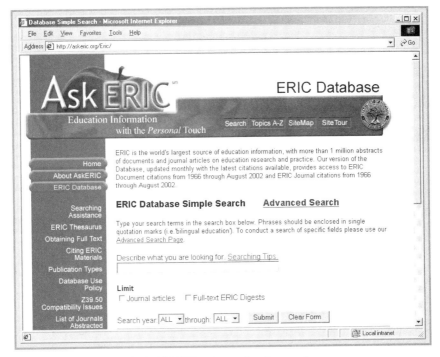

Figure 6.11: *ERIC* Database simple search screen.

from different online services, the way in which you search the database differs depending on what service you are using. So if you're accustomed to searching EBSCO*host* databases, it might be easier for you to search ERIC via EBSCO*host* than to struggle with an unfamiliar user interface.

Ingenta

The Ingenta Web site at *www.ingenta.com* provides access to a commercial database that indexes over 27,000 periodicals. Another database called *UnCover* is now a part of ingenta, which is why the screen displayed in figure 6.13, allows you to search either "online articles" or "uncover plus." While it is freely available to anyone with access to

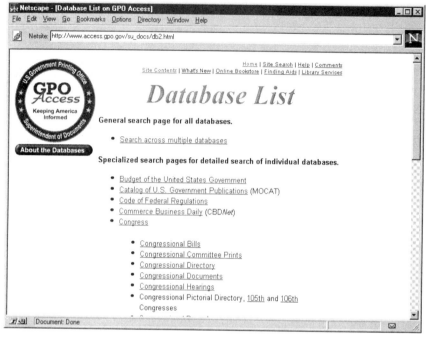

Figure 6.12: GPO Access database list.

the Web, acquiring the text of the articles entails a fee. While many of the articles can be e-mailed, there are also many in "uncover plus" that must be faxed. If you don't have time for interlibrary loan or can't go to another library and you desperately need an article, Ingenta is a good "last resort." The fees, averaging fifteen to twenty dollars, can be somewhat hefty for college students struggling to pay for pizza and gas, not to mention textbooks. But Ingenta is also useful as a Web search engine, because its "subject area resources" provides links to many free Web sites.

OK—that's enough! Your head must be spinning. There are certainly other databases that I have not covered here, but this book is not intended to turn you into a librarian. Being familiar with the major online services you are likely to encounter is sufficient and can help you understand the

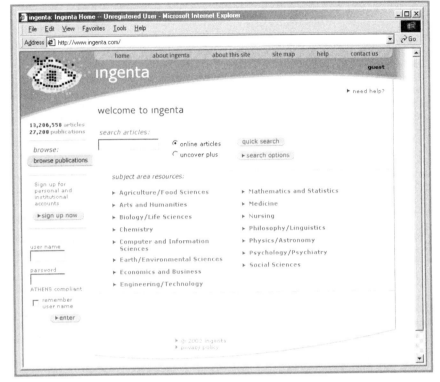

Figure 6.13: Ingenta homepage

other lesser-known ones that may also be available in your library. Just as there are many different modes of transportation (cars, trucks, buses, trains, motorcycles, SUVs, and so on), there are different resources for different research topics. Each serves a purpose, and each must be chosen with your particular needs in mind.

Seven

Use the Vehicle:
Searching Electronic Resources

Now that you're familiar with the different "makes" and "models" of databases, it's time to start the engine and take a test drive. Many of the principles explained in Chapter 2 apply here because an online book catalog is basically just another kind of database. You already know the basics of searching computerized indexes from Chapter 5. Most students never get beyond the basic search screens and simple keyword searching. They just accept the results they get and make the best of it. But advanced searching allows you to really focus in on your topic. It's like taking a good photograph: you look through the viewfinder and get just the right angle; then you bring the picture into focus. So don't settle in a figurative way for fuzzy, off-center snapshots.

In this chapter, we will focus on some more advanced searching techniques, while also reviewing some of the principles already discussed and how they can be applied to a variety of resources. Although the emphasis of this chapter will be on indexes, many of the principles apply to any type of searchable database, including the World Wide Web.

ACCESSING DATABASES

Before you can search a database for information, you must be able to access it. So the first step in using database resources is to find out which ones you have at your disposal. In many cases, you can just go to your library's Web site and see what's available. Often there will be a link on the homepage to the part of the site that lists the individual online databases the library subscribes to. This link may be called a variety of things: "electronic resources," "online databases," "computerized indexes," and so on. If your library doesn't have too many resources, the databases may all be listed on the homepage. Library Web sites are as unique as each library, so if you have any problems navigating, consult a librarian. Remember, however, that some databases may be accessible only on-campus even if there are links to them; others may require you to enter a password. Also be aware that CD-ROMs and online resources that are not Web-based may be available only for use within the library.

Some online services allow you to search in more than one database at a time. Dialog@CARL lets you select up to six databases to search simultaneously. In libraries that allow end users full access to all of FirstSearch, you can select the most appropriate databases by doing a broad search in several of them; the estimated number of records found is given for each database so you can choose those that contain the most information. In EBSCO*host*, you simply check off all the sources that you want to search on the initial listing. So if *Academic Search* and *MasterFile* are both relevant to your research, you may want to search them together.

SEARCHING DATABASES

Once you've accessed a desired database, it's time to search. This section will outline many of the features common to all databases, including a review of some of the principles discussed in Chapter 2. Although you may want to find articles written by the same author or an article with a particular title, the most frequent way of searching an electronic index is by subject or keyword. There is also a method known as natural language searching that is really just a variation on keyword searching.

Subject Versus Keyword Searching

There are no standard subject headings used to classify articles as in the *Library of Congress Subject Headings* for books. Each online service and sometimes even individual databases have their own terminology. This can make subject searching, except for simple topics, somewhat difficult. Some databases even have special names for the subject heading field: *PsycINFO* has descriptors; *Medline* has MESHs (medical subject headings), and so on.

A good example of the inconsistency of subject headings is provided by the cover story from the August 1999 *U.S. News & World Report* entitled "Schools Turn Off the Tap," which concerns steps being taken by colleges to curtail binge drinking. Notice the comparison between the headings given to the same article in two different databases.

In EBSCO*host's Academic Search*:

drinking of alcoholic beverages—universities and colleges
universities and colleges—social life and customs
college students—alcohol use

In InfoTrac's *Expanded Academic ASAP*:

alcohol—usage
fraternal organizations—social aspects
universities and colleges—alcohol use

Because of these inconsistencies, I suggest you start with keyword searching unless your topic is very straightforward.

If you're looking for articles about a certain person or place, for example, there are usually not many variations. You can also enter a broad topic and then browse through the sub-headings for that subject.

As with searching for books, determining the appropriate subject headings is still the best way to get a comprehensive listing of relevant articles. Keyword searching presents the problems of finding irrelevant material or not finding all the relevant material. But even if you find just one really good article through keyword searching, you can take a look at the subject headings given the article and backtrack, clicking on an appropriate heading. For example, let's say you wanted to find articles about binge drinking on college campuses. If you enter **college campuses and binge drinking** as your keyword search in EBSCO*host*'s *Academic Search*, 17 records are retrieved, the first few of which are displayed in Figure 7.1.

Figure 7.1: Records retrieved in EBSCO*host*'s *Academic Search Premier* for a search on **college campuses and binge drinking**.

The third is titled "Challenging the Collegiate Rite of Passage." You retrieve that citation and view the record shown in Figure 7.2.

Notice the subject headings for this article. **College students—Alcohol use—United States** sounds like a relevant subject. Since this heading is actually a Web link, you can click on it and retrieve all the articles on that subject. By doing this, you come up with a much larger set of articles. So always look at the headings of appropriate articles. They could lead you to a gold mine of related information.

Natural Language Searching

Natural language searching is a method of searching in which you simply type in a question as you would ask it. For example: "What are the effects of television violence on

Figure 7.2: Full record for an article in EBSCO*host*'s *Academic Search Premier*.

children?" Although this might make you feel like you are on the bridge of the starship *Enterprise*, what is actually happening is quite simple: the computer searches for all the significant words. In the above example, the computer would do a search for *effects, television, violence,* and *children.* Usually, the connector AND is implied between terms and the resultant set of records is sorted in order of relevancy so the records containing the highest occurrence of the search words are at the top of the list.

In some databases that allow natural language searching, the order of words in the question is important and even the insignificant words such as *the, of,* and *what* are used to determine the context of the other words. This can be a somewhat imprecise method of searching that may work well for some topics, but often retrieves irrelevant results for others.

Broadening Your Search

Searching the Full Text

If you haven't found many articles and need more information, you can broaden your search in many databases by searching the complete text of available articles. Most databases automatically limit their searches to the citation and abstract. Be forewarned, however, that full-text searching increases your chances of finding irrelevant material much more so than when only the abstract is searched. One of your search terms may be mentioned only in passing and have very little to do with the main focus of the article. An article about fraternities, for example, might mention binge drinking, while the article is really about the history of fraternities.

If you look at the opening search screen for EBSCO*host* in the last chapter (Figure 6.1), you will see that you can click on the option "search within full text articles" on the right side of the screen. In InfoTrac's keyword search mode, as displayed in Figure 7.3, the default is searching "in title,

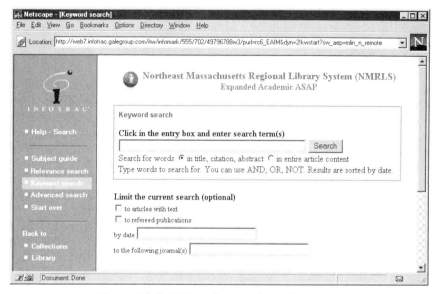

Figure 7.3: InfoTrac's keyword search mode.

citation, abstract," but you can change this to "in entire article content."

Using OR and Truncation

Since Boolean searching is applicable in just about any searchable database, another way of expanding your search is to think of synonyms for your terms and link them with the connector OR that, as you'll recall, searches for any of the terms entered. You will either have to type in the word OR between terms or, in some databases, select it from a pull-down menu. Truncation is a variation on this method. By entering the appropriate symbol at the end of a word, all variant endings will be found. Because this symbol differs, and in some databases variant endings are searched for automatically, you should refer to the "help" section of the database to find out what to do (most databases provide in-depth instructions on truncation and many other features—just look for the word *help* on the screen and click it).

Narrowing Your Search

Using Limiters

You can also limit your search in very specific ways if you have found too much. The following are limiters that are commonly available in many databases:

- Limiting by Periodical—You might have a specific journal in mind; most databases allow you to search a single periodical. This is extremely narrow, however. Before doing this, you will want to find out if the database does, indeed, index the source you are interested in. You can usually find a list of the sources covered online. In EBSCO*host*, for example, there is a "Publications" button to click on the top of the page.
- Limiting by Date—There is often the option of searching only a certain date or range of dates.
- Limiting to Articles with Full Text—In databases that contain the complete text for only selected articles, you can limit your results by searching for only the citations that also have the text. Even though this makes things easier for you, however, just be aware that you might be missing some wonderful sources.
- Limiting to Peer-Reviewed Journals—One final limiter in a number of databases that index academic journals, including *Expanded Academic ASAP* and *Academic Search*, is limiting to "peer-reviewed" publications. This will find articles only in scholarly journals that are refereed, meaning that an article must be accepted for publication by a group of scholars.

If you refer back to Figure 7.3, you can see the limiters available in InfoTrac. You can limit to full-text or peer-reviewed publications by simply clicking the appropriate boxes, or specify a date or periodical title.

Using AND and NOT

You can also narrow your search by using the Boolean connectors AND or NOT. Just to review, connect terms with AND if you want to find all of them or with NOT if you want to exclude a term. In many databases, the term AND is implied between terms; in others, you still have to enter it or select it from a pull-down menu. To add to the confusion, sometimes AND NOT or BUT NOT is used instead of simply NOT. If the specifics of how to search a database are not obvious on the search screen, they will probably be explained in greater detail in the "help" section.

Proximity Operators

In addition to Boolean connectors, you can also use something called a *proximity operator*, which allows you to narrow your search by specifying that two or more words appear within a certain number of words of each other. Proximity operators are usually composed of the letter *n* for "near" or *w* for "within" and then a number to specify the number of words. You place the proximity operator between the words that are to be searched. For example, **television n5 violence** in InfoTrac will find "television violence" as well as "violence in movies and television" because the term **violence** can appear before or after **television**. **Television w5 violence**, however, specifies that the word **violence** must occur no more than five words *after* **television**. Depending on what database you are in, the proximity operators and their use may differ. So once again, consult those "help" files to find out.

Field-Specific Searching

Just like a book record, any database record is composed of fields—the individual pieces of information that describe the item. In the case of a periodical article, these fields would include:

- author
- article title—or headline in the case of a newspaper article
- periodical title—sometimes referred to as the source
- subject headings—also commonly referred to as descriptors
- abstract—a summary of the article
- text—if available; some databases designate a separate field for the lead paragraph of an article. This is helpful for searching purposes because if your keywords appear in the first paragraph, it is likely they are not just passing references; therefore, the articles retrieved when searching the lead paragraph will be more relevant than those found searching the entire article.

Generally, when you do a basic keyword search, the entire citation as well as the abstract for each record in the database are searched automatically, even though the chances of retrieving irrelevant articles are increased if the abstracts are searched. Limiting your search to certain fields in the records can be effective in focusing your search and reducing the number of irrelevant articles you find.

When you go to the advanced searching screen in InfoTrac, displayed in Figure 7.4, you will see a form that includes a pull-down menu. The menu lets you choose which "index" to search (*index* in this context means the same thing as *field*). You can choose the basic "keyword," which will do a standard search for your term in the citations and abstracts, or "title," which will find only those records that contain your term in the articles' titles. Another option is searching by "text word," which is the same as searching the complete text of the article for your terms.

There are two types of subject searches: either "subject (su)" or "subject list (su=)." The first type of search will retrieve any articles that have subject headings containing the search term specified, but not necessarily beginning with that term. "Subject list," on the other hand, will put you in the alphabetically arranged subject-heading list at the point you

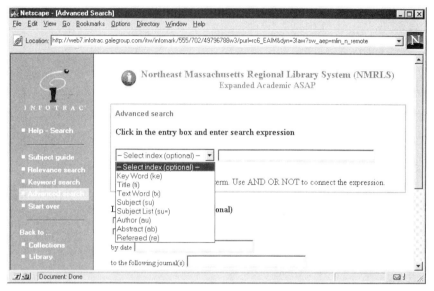

Figure 7.4: Advanced searching in InfoTrac.

specify. To differentiate, let's say you entered **alcohol** as a subject search. This would find any article that contains the term **alcohol** in any of the subject headings. This would include articles with the heading **alcohol—usage** as well as **universities and colleges—alcohol use**. If you entered this same term as a subject list search, however, you would retrieve a list of subject headings beginning with the word **alcohol** that you could then select from to retrieve articles.

The subject list can be helpful for cross references. If you look up **adolescents** in this list, for example, you would be instructed to use **teenagers** instead, since this is the official heading. Many databases have this sort of feature—some call it a thesaurus. It's a way of determining what subject headings can be used. It's a bit like looking up Library of Congress headings in the "red books."

In InfoTrac you can also limit your search to the author field in the pull-down menu or to the abstract. If you wanted to find all the articles indexed by *Expanded Academic ASAP* that were written by Carl Sagan, for example, you would go to the advanced search screen, select "author" from the pull-down menu, and then enter Sagan Carl and press "search."

Fields that can be searched differ in just about every database depending on what would be useful to the searcher. If you were searching the newspaper *USA Today* in Dialog@CARL, you could search for terms in the headline, lead paragraph, complete text, byline, dateline, or section heading. In Dialog@CARL's *SEC Online—Annual Reports* database, which provides the text of public company annual reports, searchable fields include company name, description of business, and ticker symbol.

Combining Field-Specific Searches

If your topic is at all complex, you will benefit by combining a number of field-specific searches. Consider a topic like the abuse of drugs and alcohol among adolescents. Sure, you could do a keyword search for the main terms, but as I hope I have made clear, keyword searching is often inferior to subject searching. Because there is no single subject heading to define this topic, go to InfoTrac's advanced search screen. Figure 7.5 displays the search for this topic. The bottom half of the screen shows the "history" of the search with the first part on the bottom.

First, select the subject index (su) from the pull-down menu and enter **drugs or alcohol** as your search expression in the box. This will find any articles that have the terms **drugs** or **alcohol** anywhere in the subject-heading field. Remember, the subject headings don't actually have to start with these terms. This set (R1) contains a hefty and unmanageable 15,477 articles. Next, look up **adolescents** in the subject list (su=) since you're not sure if this is a valid subject heading. Another screen pops up informing you that **teenagers** is the appropriate term to use; select that heading and you will be returned to the advanced search screen. **Teenagers** creates a second set, R2, with 4,824 citations. Then search for **abuse** in the subject index, which creates

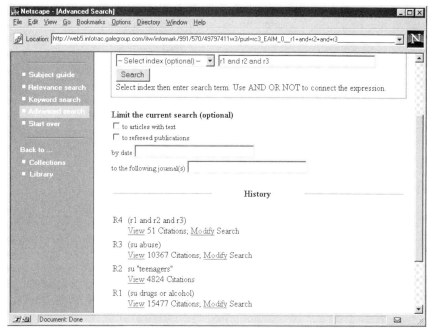

Figure 7.5: An advanced search for **drug** and
alcohol abuse among **adolescents**.

set R3 with 10,367 records. Now it's time to combine all the
sets, creating a fourth set that contains only those records
that have the terms **abuse**, and **drugs** or **alcohol** somewhere
in the subject headings, as well as the distinct subject heading **teenagers**. This resultant set is 51 highly relevant articles. Just about every database lets you perform a variation
of this technique.

A REVIEW OF THE DIRECTIONS

Perhaps you're feeling a bit overwhelmed and slightly lost
at this point, especially after my final example. That's okay.
I told you that this chapter would cover some advanced
searching techniques. I'll admit what I've covered is a bit

daunting, and I wouldn't expect you to remember how to do it all. It's beneficial just to be aware of what you could do. It's like cruise control in a car—you might never use it, but it's nice to have it anyway. In a nutshell, here are the main points you should remember:

- Find out what databases are available at your library (via your library's Web site or ask a librarian). Choose the most appropriate database for your research needs; if you don't find enough in that database, you can always try another.
- If your topic is broad or straightforward, start with a subject search; otherwise try a basic keyword search. If you've found a manageable set of records (I prefer less than 50), browse through the first screen of titles and check to see that most of them are relevant. Take a closer look at the full records for the items that sound best. If any subject heading looks particularly applicable, do a new search using this heading (usually all you have to do is click on it).
- If you've come up with records that don't seem to be relevant, revise your search using different keywords and try again.
- If you haven't found enough records, broaden your search by:
  a) entering additional terms and connecting them with OR,
  b) using truncated terms,
  c) searching the full text of records, not just the citation and abstract.
- If you've found too many records, narrow your search by:
  a) using limiters to specify a certain periodical, date, and so on,
  b) entering additional terms, and connecting them with AND,
  c) excluding a term using NOT.

- You can further refine your search by limiting it to certain fields in the record and by combining two or more field-specific searches. This often requires you to go to an advanced search screen.

Unless you're really into cars, you don't know how to deal with every mechanical problem. But it's good to know some of the basics like changing a tire. In the same way, don't feel that you have to be become an expert at searching every database. It's more practical to focus on one— preferably the one that will cover the majority of your research needs such as *Expanded Academic ASAP* or *Academic Search*. When the need arises for you to use another, more specific, database, you can always ask a librarian for help just as you can go to a mechanic when your car is in need of repair.

Eight

Explore Uncharted Territory:
The World Wide Web

Considering the metaphors I have used throughout this book, the cliché of the "information superhighway" is hard to avoid when discussing the World Wide Web. There are ways in which this image is accurate and other ways in which it seems completely wrong. The Web certainly has the potential to provide the user with a wealth of quick information, but the reality is that it also has road-blocks of its own. The attitude of this chapter is, therefore, "proceed with caution." Don't rely on the Web alone for your research paper.

This chapter will provide only a brief introduction to the immensity of the World Wide Web. Entire books have been written about how to use the Web. These books quickly go out of date because the details they cover inevitably become obsolete. Similarly, the chapter about the Internet that ap-peared in the first edition of this book bears very little re-semblance to this chapter. Therefore, my focus here will be on general principles that will probably not change too much rather than the specifics that probably will.

THE STATE OF THE WEB

The terms "World Wide Web" and "Internet" are used almost interchangeably today. But the Internet came first. The Web can be considered as simply a way of using the Internet. What we know as the Internet began in 1969 as the ARPAnet project of the Department of Defense. What emerged from this project was a worldwide network of computers—an "internet." Until the mid-1990s and the emergence of the Web, the Internet was a user-unfriendly system with no graphics. The unbelievable growth in the popularity of the Internet is due, in part, to the development of the Web as a graphical way of using this computer network.

The main problems with the Web are its disorganization, preponderance of useless information, and excessive advertising. Picture a big library in which the books are not arranged by call number, just sort of grouped together loosely by subject. This can make it difficult to find the exact location of the material you need. Also, there are no librarians selecting books for quality; anything and everything is thrown in—elementary school compositions and high school book reports along with excerpts from doctoral dissertations and works by Pulitzer Prize-winning authors. In addition, you are bombarded with advertising as "e-commerce," rather than the sharing of knowledge, seems to emerge as the Web's reason for being.

Much of what you find on the Web, you find accidentally. If you are looking for something specific, you can often become quite frustrated. Using the Web also presents technical problems. You may click on a link only to find that a resource is not found or no longer available. A Web site may be available one day and gone the next. Graphics may take a long time to load. Response time may also be slow because too many users are trying to access the same site. I don't mean to sound completely negative. I have found some wonderful information on the Web and consider it, at its best, to be an amazing source of information.

THE STRUCTURE OF THE WEB

Think of the Web once again like a library full of books. Each Web site is like one book. Just as a book has a table of contents, a Web site has a *homepage*—an introductory page from which to begin your exploring. Most Web sites consist of more than one page. Your school's homepage probably allows you to connect to all the different departmental pages, as well as pages about events, services, and the library. *Page* is a misleading term because the Web does not confine the designer of a Web site to a certain amount of space. Pages can be of all different lengths. A page on the Web is defined as the space that you can scroll through at a particular address.

In addition to providing information, most Web pages also contain *links* to other Web pages. You can access other pages by clicking on these hypertext links. Links can be either highlighted text or a graphical image. To extend our book metaphor, let's say you're looking in a book for information on your topic. You could read the book from cover to cover in a linear fashion, or you could check the index in the back of the book to determine which pages contain the specific information you need and then turn to those pages. While looking in the index, you might see related topics listed with their appropriate page numbers. Referring to these different pages and flipping back and forth in a book using the index is the hypertextual way to read. But the Web takes it a step further. Imagine looking in the bibliography at the end of a book and instantly being able to get your hands on some of the sources cited. This is the sort of thing that Web page links allow you to do.

You use browsing software to view Web sites. *Netscape* and Microsoft's *Internet Explorer* are the most popular Web browsers. The screenshots in this book provide examples of both. Depending on which browser you use, the same Web page might look slightly different if viewed from two computers using different software. But, just as two different editions of *Moby-Dick* might look different but contain exactly the same text, the content of the Web site remains the same.

THE CONTENT OF THE WEB

The Web resources that are the focus of this chapter differ from most of the other Web-based sources in this book because they are freely accessible to anyone who has access to the Web. In a figurative sense, no toll is required. As with just about anything that appears to be free, however, there are often hidden costs in the form of advertising and propaganda.

What can you find on the Web? That's like asking what you can see on a cross-country road trip. Because of the sheer bulk of information available, only some broad generalizations can be offered here based on the categories of information providers.

- Companies provide a lot of information about their products and services on the Web; mostly this is just advertising, but sometimes such information can be helpful. If you're researching a company, you will certainly want to take a look at its Web site. With the rise of "e-commerce," many commercial sites are not only sources of information but interactive sites where customers can purchase products and perform transactions.
- Nonprofit organizations also have a strong presence on the Web. These organizations are formed to promote a cause, so their sites are designed to help in their mission. No matter how altruistic this mission is, watch out for propaganda and bias when viewing these sites. They're certainly not out to make a buck the way the commercial sites blatantly are, but they often have an agenda.
- Educational institutions—practically every college and

university has a Web site now. Many secondary schools and even elementary schools are going online with their own sites as well. Access to your library's Web-based resources is usually provided through your school's site. In addition to lots of information about events, student services, courses, and individual departments, colleges often let students and faculty post their own personal pages. While these can be excellent sources for research, be careful to evaluate the material as detailed in the next chapter. You might have at your disposal the wisdom of a world-renowned expert in Shakespearean studies who has made his research available to the world with no thought of financial gain. Or, at the other end of the spectrum, you might be able to view a fraternity site that explains how to make your own beer.

- U.S. government departments and agencies have always had a strong presence in cyberspace, ever since the Internet originated back in the late 1960s as a project of the Department of Defense. As mentioned in Chapter 4, governmental sites can be wonderful, objective sources of information and provide lots of statistics, reports, and so on.
- Personal Web sites can often be identified by a tilde (~) in the address. This category of site can be the biggest offender in the amount of junk on the Web. Although the other categories of sites usually have some form of editorial control because there is a higher organization to which the Web page author has to answer, personal pages can contain anything from pornography to cookie recipes. Be extremely cautious when using personal sites, and make sure that the original source of any secondary information is clearly cited.

FINDING INFORMATION ON THE WEB

Web Addresses

Addresses, also sometimes called URLs or *uniform resource locators*, are entered in the location box of your browser in order to access a particular Web page. These addresses often begin with *www*, but this is no longer required. You also see Web addresses that begin with http://, but you can omit this when entering the URL. The domain name, the first part of the address that takes you to a homepage, ends with one of the following codes (called top-level domains) that give an indication of the source of the information:

- **.com**—commercial sites; two new top-level domains are **.pro**, for doctors, lawyers, and other professionals, and **.biz**.
- **.org**—nonprofit organizations (there is a new specific top-level domain **.museum** for—you guessed it—museums).
- **.edu**—educational institutions.
- **.gov**—government agencies (the related top-level domain **.mil** specifies a military site).
- **.net**—Internet service providers, which are companies that provide access to the Web (personal Web sites often have this top-level domain).
- **.name**—a new top-level domain for the personal Web sites of individuals.
- **.info**—a new general top-level domain for individual sites, businesses, or organizations.

Specific addresses for pages in a Web site beyond the homepage are lengthier and often more complicated with backslashes to separate each portion of the URL. For example, the address for an episode guide to the television show *Friends* is *www.nbc.com/Friends/episode_guide/index.html*. If you entered just the domain name, *www.nbc.com*, you would access the homepage of NBC, from which you could select *Friends* or another one of this network's shows. If you entered *www.nbc.com/Friends*, you would go to the *Friends* homepage within the NBC site from which you could select the episode guide. But if you enter the entire address, you would go directly to the episode guide itself.

The address for a Web page is equivalent to the call number for a book and is often structured hierarchically like a call number. If you know the address, you can easily find the source. You can obtain Web site addresses from a variety of sources—magazines, books, TV commercials, librarians, professors, friends, acquaintances, and so on. The other way to access Web sites is to click on hypertext *links*.

"Surfing"

Surfing is basically a process of clicking on Web page links. As an example of surfing, take a look at Figure 8.1, a page from NASA's Web site that gives a brief history of the ill-fated Apollo 13 mission.

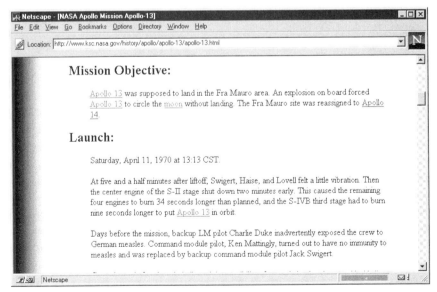

Figure 8.1: A portion of a page from NASA's Web site.

Notice in the second line under "Mission Objective" that the word *moon* is highlighted. When you click on this highlighted term, you can immediately access a Web site with information about the moon, as displayed in Figure 8.2. This doesn't just happen automatically. The designer of the NASA Web site decided to link to this other site.

This Web site has nothing to do with NASA; it's maintained by a software engineer named Bill Arnett who lives in Arizona and is interested in astronomy. From this site, if you were to click on the name *Artemis*, which is highlighted, you'll be taken to another Web site at an altogether different location that discusses Greek mythology. This is the nature of hypertext and what makes the Web so enticing. Although it gives you the freedom to jump around and follow various topics that may only have loose connections, it's really just like wandering around a library that isn't organized very well and haphazardly opening up books.

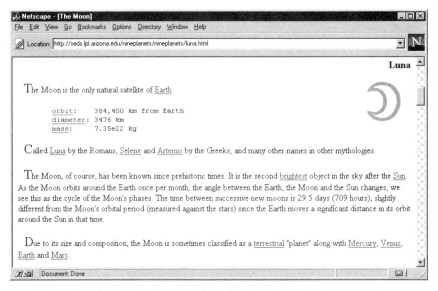

Figure 8.2: A portion of a page from "The Nine Planets: A Multimedia Tour of the Solar System" by Bill Arnett.

Table 8.1: Tools For Searching the Web

- **About.com** (*www.about.com*)—a subject directory where searches can be limited to the sites chosen by expert human "guides" in over 700 subject areas or broadened to include sites not in the directory.

- **AlltheWeb** (*www.alltheweb.com*)—a large engine covering over two billion pages

- **AltaVista** (*www.altavista.com*)—a medium-sized search engine that covers half a billion pages.

- **Ask Jeeves** (*www.ask.com*)—a search service using natural language searching as well as related search terms based on the searches of previous users.

- **Dogpile** (*www.dogpile.com*)—a metasearch engine that simultaneously searches About, Ask Jeeves, Google, Overture, and others.

- **Google** (*www.google.com*)—one of the largest search engines, covering over three billion pages; also has a very comprehensive subject directory, which is a version of Open Directory (see next page) and contains 1.5 million pages.

- **Librarians' Index to the Internet** (*www.lii.org*)—includes over 10,000 sites carefully chosen by librarians.

- **Lycos** (*www.lycos.com*)—a portal site that uses search results from AlltheWeb and directory listings from Open Directory.

- **MetaCrawler**(*www.metacrawler.com*)—a metasearch engine that searches About, Ask Jeeves, FAST, FindWhat, LookSmart, Overture, and other search engines.

Continued

Table 8.1: *Continued*

- **Open Directory** (*www.dmoz.org*)—a large subject directory compiled by volunteer editors.

- **WebCrawler** (*www.webcrawler.com*)—a metasearch engine that has very little advertising and searches major search engines such as AltaVista, Direct Hit, Looksmart, and About.

- **WorldCat** (*via FirstSearch*)—a database that includes the cataloging of Web sites according to the same principles used by libraries to catalog books, which facilitates subject access to relevent sites.

- **WWW Virtual Library** (*www.vlib.org*)—an advertising-free directory of the Web compiled by volunteers who are experts in wide range of subject areas.

- **Yahoo!** (*www.yahoo.com*)—one of the oldest directories on the Web; retrieves sites found in the Yahoo subject directory first, then sponsors that pay for placement, then Web sites found by Google outside the directory.

Search Engine Overview

Web sites that are specifically designed to help you find other sites are called *search engines*. Using search engines to find Web sites can loosely be compared to using an online catalog to find books. The purpose of this section is not to explain how to use each one. That would be quite futile considering how much they change, and also impossible considering the sheer number of them. There are close to three thousand search engines listed at *searchengineguide.com*! But I would like you to understand the common features that the major search engines share, as well as some of the unique features that distinguish them. Table 8.1 gives you an overview of the major search engines and other Web-based tools that help you find sites. A great place to go to find out the latest developments and news about search engines is *www.searchenginewatch.com*.

Despite the variety of search engines, they all provide a search box in which you can enter your terms, and, in return, get a list of links to sites that contain these terms. Unfortunately, most search engines are becoming so filled with shopping guides and other commercial material that it's hard to know exactly what to do once you get to one of them. Take a look, for example, at the homepage of Lycos displayed in Figure 8.3.

Figure 8.3: Lycos homepage.

The search box almost gets lost in the screen, as the user is enticed by the chance to win a trip to Hawaii, find a job, or get a free tote bag. There is also a consumer-oriented subject guide on the left side of the screen and services like e-mail, chat, horoscopes, and personal ads. Search engines that incorporate a variety of resources and services, including Web directories, free e-mail, news, chat rooms, and online shopping, are called *portal sites*. The emphasis of these portals seems to be on commercial purposes rather than academic research. You can get distracted by all the opportunities to buy things, chat with people, and check out the latest news.

In contrast to this, take a look at the Google homepage displayed in Figure 8.4.

It is refreshing to see a Web search engine homepage that is so uncluttered. Advertising does appear on Google search result pages, but these links to sponsor sites are text-only and

Figure 8.4: Google homepage.

unobtrusive. Google has emerged since the last edition of this book as one of the most popular search engines because of the relevancy of its results, and also, I believe, because of the low-key advertising.

Search Engine Directories

Although I compared search engines to online book catalogs, there is a major difference. Records in an online catalog have a standard format and are assigned subject headings, which make it easy to access all of the items on a certain topic once you have determined what the appropriate headings are. But you generally enter keywords in search engines; as always, this means that your searching will be imprecise. OCLC's *WorldCat*, the FirstSearch database highlighted in Chapter 6, has begun cataloging Web sites in the same manner that it does books and other material in an attempt to create an online catalog for the Web that classifies sites under Library of Congress subject headings.

To provide a way to access sites by subject, many search engines now have directories that arrange sites hierarchically into various categories so you can browse if your topic is fairly broad rather than enter keywords in the search box. This is as close as search engines come to assigning subject headings to sites, but there is no uniformity to these directories. If you refer back to Figure 8.3, you will see that Lycos has a Web Directory providing a number of consumer-oriented categories.

The popular Yahoo!, one of the oldest directories on the Web, categorizes over one million Web sites under a small number of main headings listed in its directory. You can see part of this directory on the homepage displayed in Figure 8.5, at the bottom left portion of the screen. To see the entire directory you have to scroll down the page a bit, or, better yet, enter the address *dir.yahoo.com* to access a Web page that contains the directory alone without much advertising or other clutter.

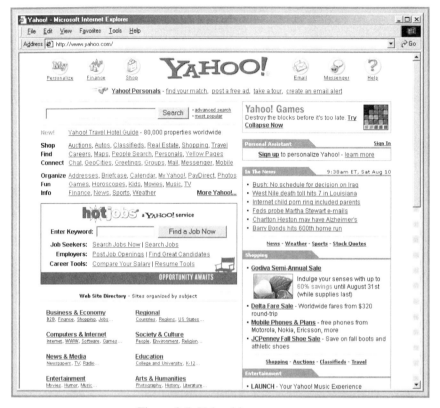

Figure 8.5: Yahoo! homepage.

Clicking on one of Yahoo!'s main headings will bring you to another page that lists the subheadings for the chosen topic. For example, let's say you wanted to take a look at the Web sites of various modern art museums. Click on the first category in the directory, "Arts & Humanities." This brings up the screen displayed in Figure 8.6.

From this screen select "Museums, Galleries, and Centers." The next screen to appear is shown in Figure 8.7, which lists narrower subheadings, including "Modern and Contemporary."

Notice that below the list of subheadings, links to indi-

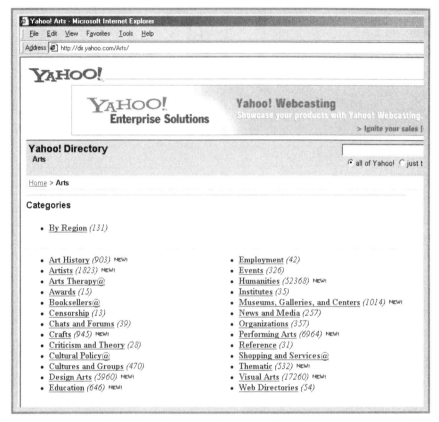

Figure 8.6: Yahoo! "Arts & Humanities" directory.

vidual museums have appeared. Click on any of these and you will go to the site of the museum listed. These links fit into many different categories. But because you specifically want to view the links for modern art museums, you would have to select that option from the list of headings at the top portion of the screen. This would bring you to a page that provides links to numerous modern art museums. The first ten links are to the most popular sites; this is followed by an alphabetical listing of all the other museums.

Figure 8.7: Yahoo! "Museums, Galleries, and Centers" directory.

What Are You Searching?

At this point it is important to understand that there is no search engine that covers the entire Web. Even metasearch engines, which are sites allowing you to search multiple engines simultaneously, don't cover every single page. Each engine covers a different range of sites just as each online catalog covers a different collection of resources, but there is definitely overlap among search engines, just as there is overlap among periodical indexes. There are also cooperative agreements between search engines. Yahoo! uses

Google's search results for searches outside the directory; Lycos uses search results from AlltheWeb and directory listings from Open Directory. This is similar to the way in which some of the database providers described in Chapter 6 provide access to databases not produced by them.

There are two ways that search engines select the sources to be covered. Sites can be evaluated by human beings for inclusion in a directory. Yahoo!, for example, employs a team of people to find acceptable sites and then assign a category to each one. Yahoo! also accepts submissions from users, which are evaluated by their team for inclusion. Search engines that allow you to search outside the limited scope of a human-compiled subject directory automate the whole process of selection by sending out electronic "spiders" to go to sites and add them to the database. Then the spiders follow all the links on the initial sites and add all of those secondary sites, and so on. Some search engines that boast the number of pages they index rely on quantity rather than quality. This difference is important when it comes to evaluating the results of your search.

The lesson to be learned is that if your topic is somewhat broad, you might want to use a search engine's directory that covers fewer sites and employs some selection criteria. On the other hand, if your topic is a bit more obscure, you may want to start by entering keywords in the search box.

Searching Techniques

Much of what you learned about searching a database in Chapters 2 and 7 relates to searching the Web, so I won't give a lot of examples in this section. Each search engine is a little different. Most have "help" pages that provide you with tips and examples to highlight their unique features. Like just about all the databases we've seen in this book, there are both basic and advanced ways of using Web search engines. But the average search engine user never gets beyond entering a string of keywords in the search box and then browsing through a list of links that can often contain irrelevant sites.

First of all, you can use Boolean connecting terms in most Web search engines. The ways in which you do this differ from engine to engine. But generally, if you enter a string of keywords, the term AND is implied between them in most of the major search engines. So the more keywords you enter, the fewer results you will get and the more precise your search will be. Because the term AND is implied, an almost universal rule is that, in order to find an exact phrase, you enter it within quotation marks (some search engines allow you to select "exact phrase" as an option either in a pull-down menu or a checkbox). If you were looking for sites about the singer Faith Hill and entered **Faith Hill** in a search engine without quotation marks, you would retrieve all the sites that contain the words *faith* and *hill*, so many of these would be irrelevant.

To make sure a search engine finds a particular term, some search engine help screens advise you to put a plus sign (+) before the word (although most of the search engines I "noodled" with retrieved the same results whether or not I did this). Some search engines ignore common words like prepositions (*at, to, from*, and so on) and other short words (*where, what, that*, and so on), so if you really want these words to be a part of your search, put a plus sign in front of them. Also, if for some reason you want the words *and, or*, or *not* to be search terms rather than Boolean connectors, use the plus sign. What I find more useful is the minus sign (–) to signify NOT, which eliminates a term from your search. For example, if you entered the following search: **Titanic –"Leonardo DiCaprio"** in just about any of the search engines, you will increase your chances of finding sites concerned with the demise of the real ship rather than Leonardo DiCaprio fan club sites and other sites concerned with the Oscar-winning film.

You can also use the connecting term OR to broaden your search in many search engines. But be careful because some

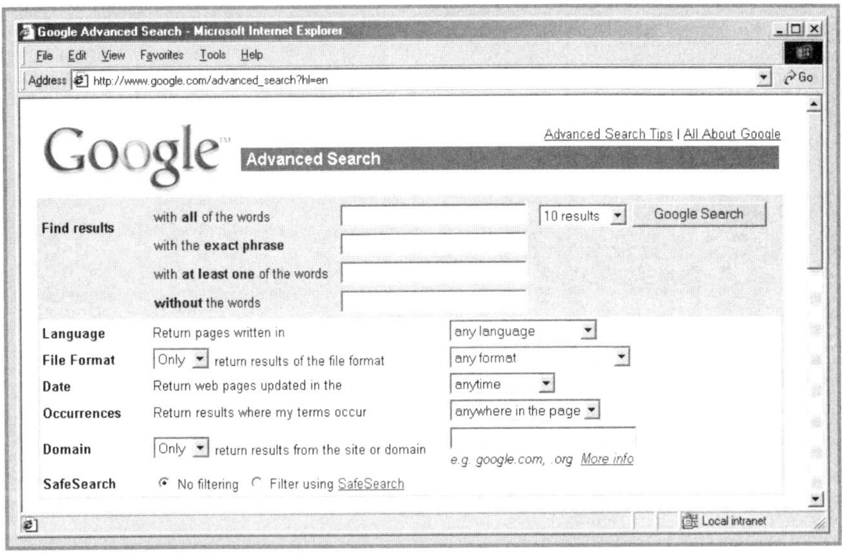

Figure 8.8: Google advanced search page.

search engines, such as AltaVista, consider *or* a keyword rather than a connecting term. Most Web search engines do not support truncation, so if you want to find the variant endings of a search term, it is best to enter each variation connected by OR in search engines that allow this.

Most search engines have an advanced search page that facilitates the searching process. As you can see in Figure 8.8, Google provides a more detailed search form that simplifies Boolean searching by letting you find sites "with all of the words" (AND), "with the exact phrase," "with at least one of the words" (OR), or "without the words" (NOT). It also lets you limit your search by language, date updated, and allows you to specify whether you want to find the terms in the title of the site, which can help retrieve more relevant sites, or the full text, which will increase your results.

On the Lycos advanced search page, the options are "should include" (OR), "must include" (AND), and "must not include" (NOT). You can also limit your search to the text or the title, and by language, but not by date updated.

Natural language searching is becoming popular in Web

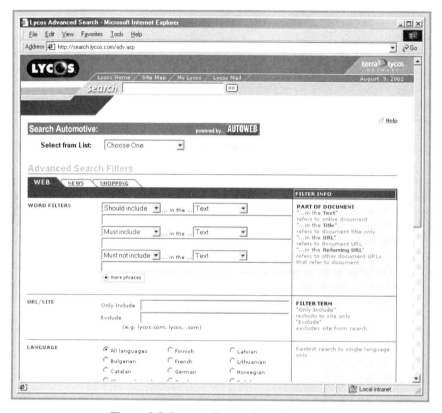

Figure 8.9: Lycos advanced search page.

search engines such as Ask Jeeves. As mentioned in the previous chapter, you enter a question to which you need an answer; the search engine searches for the prominent terms and ranks the results by relevance.

Order of Web Pages Found

When you do a keyword search in an online catalog, your list of books is usually displayed in alphabetical order. When you receive a list of Web site links in response to your search engine query, what order are they displayed in? Some search engines employ a relevancy ranking that orders sites retrieved by the frequency of search terms. In other words, sites that contain all of your words in the greatest quantity will appear at the top of the list. Other search engines rank sites by popularity so the sites that have been visited the most by other users on this topic will appear first. The reasoning is that the most useful sites will emerge since users have, in a way, voted for them.

Google employs a variation of the popularity method that has proven to be highly effective in retrieving relevant sites. Sites that are linked the most to other sites have a higher ranking. For example, if you search for **John F. Kennedy**, the first site in the results list is the JFK Library. This means that more sites about Kennedy link to the JFK Library site than to any other site. The logic here is that a site that has been chosen by the designer of another site to be included as a link must be a useful site.

Then there is a deceptive type of ranking that is tied to fees paid by Web sites to search engines. For example, Overture (formerly GoTo) allows companies to pay a fee so that their sites will appear higher in the list than others. Other search engines, such as Yahoo! and Lycos, list their "sponsor sites" first. These "pay-for-placement" sites may not be as useful in your research as noncommercial sites.

Search Engine Recommendations

I can't tell you definitively which search engine is best. There are so many, I honestly have not had time to evaluate even the major ones highlighted in this chapter as thoroughly as I'd like to. Right now, Google seems to be all the rage, but with the everchanging nature of the Web, another upstart could take its place. You will develop your own personal favorites just as I have, based on your success rate and your comfort level. It's best to choose a couple that you like—perhaps one for broad searches and one for narrower topics—and focus on learning how to use them well. Table

8.1 provides you with a list of the major search engines and other tools for finding Web sites along with their addresses and some brief notes on each.

As for my personal preferences, I like Yahoo! for subjects of a general nature or when I'm in the mood to browse a bit. For more specific searches, I have had good luck with Google. I tend to stay away from the highly consumer-oriented search engines—those with so much advertising you can hardly find the search box. I hardly ever use metasearch engines, which search multiple search engines simultaneously. I think they are best reserved for the narrowest topics; otherwise, you are likely to be overwhelmed by information.

You may find Web sites that contain pages saying "Under Construction." In a way, the entire Web is under construction, and by its nature, will always be a "work in progress," just as the highway system must continually be maintained with new roads being built and old ones paved over. The tools used to search the Web are also under construction. So, be prepared for a bumpy ride and, as I advised you in the beginning of this chapter, proceed with caution. But enjoy the ride because you will certainly see some unexpected and wonderful things.

Nine

Bring It All Back Home:
Evaluating and Citing Information

During a long road trip I like to think about where I've been and what I've seen. I might make some evaluations about what I liked and didn't like and if I'd want to travel the same route again in the future. I often feel compelled to write about my travels in order to preserve a record of the trip. In a similar way, you will benefit from evaluating the informational sources you find in your journey through the library, and the research paper you write will provide an account of your "trip."

EVALUATING WHAT YOU'VE FOUND

Doing research is not just about finding information, it's also about evaluating what you've found and determining what will be useful. This is especially critical when it comes to Web resources. With the constantly increasing amount of information available and the powerful electronic tools we now have for accessing it, you may well discover, to your surprise and dismay, that you've overwhelmed yourself with too many resources.

Although I've placed this section on evaluation here at the end of this book, evaluating your sources should actually be an ongoing process rather than something you do after you've found everything on your topic. Evaluation focuses on four main points: authority, content, accuracy, and currency. This is true for books, articles, Web sites—any information.

Authority: Who Wrote It?

An author with credentials or some sort of track record adds credibility to a resource. While you can't always find out much about the author, books usually contain brief biographies. With periodicals, remember that you don't want to rely exclusively on popular magazines. Articles from scholarly journals carry more weight and are generally written by experts in their field. Plus, these articles have often been selected by the author's peers as worthy of publication.

When it comes to evaluating the authority of Web sites, however, the problem is that anyone can put up a Web site. Many sites have absolutely no editorial control. It is important to know who is behind the information you see on a Web page. This can sometimes be more difficult than with print resources. The author is not always identified. The "Webmaster," who may be named at the bottom of the page, is not necessarily the author; rather, this person designs or maintains the site.

You can tell a lot about a Web site simply from its address. As explained in the last chapter, sites with domain names ending in *.com* are commercial sites. Such sites are usually trying to sell something; they are just advertising in disguise. Keep this in mind when evaluating the informational content of the site. If the domain name ends in *.org*, the site is put up by a nonprofit organization. Therefore, it is likely that the purpose of the site is to promote the cause of the organization. This bias will add a certain slant to the information. Sites affiliated with educational institutions have domain names ending in *.edu*. You might think that the information included in such sites would be free of propaganda, but think again. Also look out for student's personal pages. You can identify a personal page because it usually contains a tilde (~). The problem with such pages is that there is absolutely no editorial control. They may contain bad poetry, family photos, or a high school student's science paper.

Content: Does It Adequately Address My Topic?

Perhaps the most fundamental question you should ask is whether each source adequately provides you with the information you need. Does it answer the main questions you have about your topic? The records you find using indexes and online book catalogs do not always have enough information to evaluate the material cited. Even when you are given an abstract in an article citation or a table of contents in an online book record, you may not get a clear idea of what the source will really provide. The only way to do this is to get your hands on the actual book or article and skim through it, noticing how extensively your topic is addressed. You might also want to look up your topic in the book's index to get a sense of how many pages are devoted to it. Even though the source might have sounded great initially, you may realize that it won't really help you. Don't select a source for the sake of having one more item to add to your bibliography or just because it is easier to get. The quality of your information is more important than the quantity.

As I've touched upon previously, the best material may not always be the easiest information to get your hands on. For example, you might have to go to microfilm to get an old newspaper article or use a print index in order to find articles from the precomputer days. Although I certainly appreciate the information superhighway that has been created by computers, I also see the value of the informational "back roads." Even though the highway can be very useful when your primary goal is to get somewhere fast, it is often more interesting to explore the back roads when you have the time.

Accuracy: Is the Information Correct?

Accuracy is related to content and is most applicable to evaluating Web sites. A book or article should have gone through an editorial process that will have involved fact-checking, while Web sites, as I'm sure is clear by now, are often unedited and, as a result, contain a lot of erroneous information. But print resources are not perfect either. If you have found a number of articles and books and gained a working knowledge of your subject, you may have learned enough to notice inaccuracies in some of your print resources too. If you detect numerous inaccuracies in a resource, you may want to reconsider using it.

Even if you notice minor errors like misspellings, you should be cautious because this reflects poorly on the source as a whole. Here's an interesting example that points out the weakness of the Web as compared to edited print sources. Using the search engine Google, I looked up the term *millennium*, which might be a keyword you would use if researching the Y2K bug like the student in the beginning of this book. Google found nearly six million references. Then I misspelled the term as *millenium* and still found almost two million! That's an error rate of about 25 percent; for each four Web pages containing this term, one had misspelled it. This is not Google's fault, but due to the unedited content of the Web. Next, I searched for *millennium* in Infotrac's *Expanded Academic ASAP* and found 57,248 articles, while the erroneous *millenium* retrieved 4,335. The error rate for published periodicals covered by this index was much lower at about 7 percent.

Currency: When Was It Written?

Sometimes it's important to have the most recent information available, especially for scientific and business-related topics. In such cases, as you search for material on your subject, you should keep in mind the date each item was written. This will help you narrow your search and focus on the most valuable information. At other times, it is not necessary to have the most up-to-date material, particularly with historical topics or those related to the humanities. In fact, when researching such areas, the latest information may not be the best.

Most students, however, prefer more recent information, particularly periodical articles, because it is usually easier to obtain. As I pointed out, most of the older articles are on microfilm and to find citations for this material you may have to use a print index rather than an electronic one. With the increasing availability of recent full-text articles online, more people are opting for current information. While I have nothing against the convenience of full-text electronic sources, I have observed that too many students rely exclusively on the limited sources available in this format. Let me once again remind you that, just as cruising historic Route 66 is much more interesting than speeding along on Interstate 40, sometimes the most interesting sites are off the beaten track. So don't always look for the fastest way to get the most recent information. You may miss out on some really good sources.

It's easy enough to determine the date that a book was written. The copyright date will be on one of the first few left-hand pages. It will also be listed in the online catalog record. The dates for articles are included in the citations you found through indexes. Finding out how old a Web page is can be problematic (like so many things about the Web), because Web sites are constantly updated. If the Webmaster has followed the rules of good design and maintenance, the date when the site was last updated should appear prominently on the homepage as well as on each page that has been revised within the site. Even if a date does appear on a Web page, however, you often have no way of knowing if it is the date of initial creation or the date of most recent revision.

THE RECORD OF YOUR TRIP:
CITING YOUR SOURCES

Of course, the end product of all your research and the record of your trip is reflected in the paper or project that you complete for your class. This book is not intended to teach you how to actually write the paper, but an important component of your paper is the documentation that gives credit to the sources you used to write it. Students frequently ask librarians how to cite resources, so I'd like to briefly discuss this.

There is no single method of citing sources. Your professor may request that you follow a certain format. The rules laid out in *The Chicago Manual of Style*'s chapter on documentation are often specified, or your professor might suggest Kate Turabian's *A Manual for Writers of Term Papers, Theses, and Dissertations*, which follows the same rules as *Chicago*. Two other common formats are the MLA (Modern Language Association) style and the APA (American Psychological Association) style. To learn how to use these styles, refer to the following handbooks available in most libraries: *The MLA Handbook for Writers of Research Papers* and *The Publication Manual of the American Psychological Association*. Each of these four books will show you in great detail how to cite just about anything you could possibly want to cite. More recent editions include rules on citing electronic resources. No matter which style you choose, the important thing is to be consistent. In other words, if you use MLA for one citation, you must use MLA for all.

The list of sources you should include at the end of your paper is generically referred to as a bibliography. When using MLA style, however, you title this page "Works Cited," while according to APA, it is called "References." But if you're using the *Chicago* style, just call it the "Bibliography." In addition to a bibliography, you need to incorporate notes into your paper. Immediately after you use a direct quote or paraphrase the thought of someone else, you must give credit to the source—including the exact page reference.

With *Chicago* style, you use either footnotes or endnotes. A superscript number is inserted at the end of the passage you want to cite. Then you either include a citation as a footnote at the bottom of the page or collect all your citations together as endnotes at the end of the paper. Unlike bibliography citations, these are more specific, citing the exact page numbers. When using APA or MLA style, you don't use footnotes or endnotes. Instead you use parenthetical citations; for example, if you quote what Dr. Smith wrote on page 2 of his book, you just insert "(Smith, 2)" after the quote.

The purpose of citing sources is to give credit to the authors of the sources you used, to give credibility to the facts you state in your paper, and to enable anyone who reads your paper to locate these sources. It is very important to include accurate information and double-check all your citations.

In the next few pages, I'll provide you with some general guidelines on how to cite the main categories of material: books, periodical articles, and Web pages. I'll use examples that follow *Chicago* style, which seems most common in undergraduate research papers. Just consult the APA or MLA style guides if your professor prefers one or the other. And if you do use *Chicago* style, you'll need to consult *The Chicago Manual of Style* if your sources vary from the examples discussed here.

Citing Books

The basic components of a book citation are the author, the title, the publisher, and the place and date of publication. For example, here is a typical citation for a book using *The Chicago Manual of Style*:

Nelson, Rob. *Revolution X: A Survival Guide for Our Generation*. New York: Penguin Books, 1994.

Suppose that within your paper, you also quoted something written on page 95 of Nelson's book. Following *Chicago* style, you have to provide a footnote or endnote; this has a slightly different format than the bibliographic citation above:

[1]Rob Nelson, *Revolution X: A Survival Guide for Our Generation* (New York: Penguin Books, 1994), 95.

Notice that the author's name is not inverted and that the citation is indented. There are also subtle (and annoying) differences in punctuation—commas instead of periods and parentheses around the publisher and date. If you cite the same source more than once in your paper, *Chicago* style gets a little easier. Let's say that the footnote immediately following the one above cites something Nelson said on page 143. There is no need to repeat the entire citation; you would just use "ibid., 143." In case you're curious, "ibid." stands for "ibidem," which in Latin means "in the same place." If there were an intervening footnote, however, you would have to use a shortened citation omitting the subtitle and all but the most essential information: "Nelson, *Revolution X*, 143."

There are many variations for citing books: Your book may have two, three, or more authors; or no author but, instead, an editor, as in the case of many reference works. It could be a multivolume work or a specific edition. In each of these cases, the citation is a little different, so refer to *The Chicago Manual of Style* for guidance.

Citing Periodical Articles

By now you should be familiar with the basic components of a periodical article citation, since they are included in all indexes: the author, the title of the article, the title of the periodical in which the article is published, the date of the issue, page numbers, and, in the case of a journal, the volume and issue numbers.

The format for your citations, however, is a bit different from what you've seen in indexes. Here's a sample bibliographic citation and footnote for an article in a popular magazine using *The Chicago Manual of Style*:

Fischoff, Stuart. "Confessions of a TV Talk Show Shrink." *Psychology Today*, Sept./Oct. 1995, 38–45.

[1]Stuart Fischoff, "Confessions of a TV Talk Show Shrink," *Psychology Today*, Sept./Oct. 1995, 38–45.

If you are citing an article from a scholarly journal, you must also include the volume and issue numbers before the date and page numbers, so the format would follow the example below:

Wexler, Mark N. "The Psycho-Social Significance of Trivia." *Journal of Popular Culture* 28, no. 2 (1994): 1–11.

[1]Mark N. Wexler, "The Psycho-Social Significance of Trivia," *Journal of Popular Culture* 28, no. 2 (1994): 1–11.

What if you got the text of an article online, perhaps through InfoTrac or EBSCO*host*? The citation format has to reflect this. Let's say you found the *Psychology Today* article online on EBSCO*host*'s *MasterFILE Premier*. Here's how you can cite it in a bibliography using *Chicago* style:
Fischoff, Stuart. "Confessions of a TV Talk Show Shrink." *Psychology Today*, Sept./Oct. 1995, 38+. Available from *MasterFILE Premier* [online database] (Boston, MA: EBSCO Publishing) <http://search.epnet.com> (5 November 2002).

The rules regarding electronic citation are not set in stone like those for more traditional resources. Refer to the most recent edition of the style guides for more specific instructions. Some of the online databases have help screens that explain how to cite the material contained in them. In addition to the citation of the original print source of the article, you must indicate what online service you used, the location and name of the company that produces it, the Web address of the service's homepage, and the date you accessed it. Page numbers are irrelevant when it comes to Web versions of articles. But a citation for the online version of an article that originally appeared in print should indicate the page numbers for the print version. If the exact range of pages is not known, just give the first page followed by a plus sign, as in the example above.

Citing Web Pages

The rules for citing Web pages are similar to those for citing electronic versions of print articles. If you recall that one of the fundamental purposes of citing resources is so others can find them, then the information you should include makes sense. Although the rules are still under development, some general guidelines can be given here. I found a site including a page that interpreted *Chicago* style for online citations. Using the rules there, I composed the following bibliographic citation and footnote for this site:

> Harnack, Andrew, and Eugene Kleppinger. "Using Chicago Style to Cite and Document Sources." *Online!: A Reference Guide to Using Internet Sources.* 2001.<http://www.bedfordstmartins.com/online/cite7.html> (7 November 2002).

> [1]Andrew Harnack and Eugene Kleppinger, "Using Chicago Style to Cite and Document Sources," *Online!: A Reference Guide to Using Internet Sources*, 2001, <http://www.bedfordstmartins.com/online/cite7.html> (7 November 2002).

Other sites that I consulted agreed on this basic structure. As you can see I included the following:

- Author's name—basically, whoever is responsible for the content; this could be an individual or an organization. If no author is indicated, you'll just have to leave this out.
- Title of the Web page and Web site—to understand the difference, here is an analogy: a Web page is like a chapter in a book, while a Web site is like the entire book. In the above example, "Using Chicago Style to Cite and Document Sources" is the specific Web page, while *Online!: A Reference Guide to Using Internet Sources* is the name of the entire Web site. Remember a Web page's length is not confined to a certain size as a printed book is.
- Date—when the page was created (or date of most recent update).
- Address—the complete URL (be careful to double-check; sometimes these can be long).
- Date visited—when you accessed it.

LOOKING BACK DOWN THE ROAD

We've traveled a long road together since the beginning of this book. Along the way I've given you many directions, pointed out many sights, and tried to impart to you a sense of familiarity with the world of research. With this background, I hope you feel prepared to take the wheel confidently and travel through the library—both real and virtual.

Just to make sure that you're headed the right way as you finish this book, let's review the basic directions I've given for doing effective research:

- First, you need to know where you're going and what you're looking for. Define your topic. If possible, pick a topic that interests you, just as you would choose a vacation destination for its appeal. Plan your route by determining what types of sources you need, how you will find them, and roughly how much time it will take you. Don't procrastinate!

- Start by searching the online catalog for books. If you have problems with subject searching, try keyword searching using the basic principles of Boolean logic.
- Go to the stacks and locate the books whose records you found on the computer. If you need more books, do some "educated browsing" or consider using the collections of other libraries.
- Consult some basic reference sources if you need to check a fact or get some background information.
- Locate periodical articles on your topic using online and CD-ROM indexes; use print indexes for older articles.
- Determine what indexes are available at your library and in what format, then select those most appropriate for your topic.
- If you find too many articles, narrow your search; if you find too few, broaden your search using the principles outlined in Chapter 7.
- Search the Web. If you have acquired a knowledge of your topic from books and articles, you will be better able to evaluate the accuracy of Web resources. Remember, there's a lot of junk out there. The most effective way to find what you need on the Web is to use search engines, particularly the advanced search screens.

Here's a word of advice—whenever I'm lost on the road, I don't wander around too long before I stop for directions. I figure I can save a lot of time and frustration if I simply ask someone for help. In the same way, you should not hesitate to ask for help in your library. Even after reading this book, you may find there are times when you feel a bit lost. That's understandable, and that's why every library has a reference desk where you can go to find your way amid all the resources available.

EPILOGUE: RIDING OFF INTO THE SUNSET

On a road trip, you may travel hundreds, even thousands of miles for days, maybe weeks. You might think you've covered a lot of territory. But if you take a look at a globe, you'll realize how little of the world you've actually seen. Even if you spend your lifetime traveling, you'll never see it all.

It's the same with information. Consider, for example, that approximately fifty thousand books are published each year in the United States alone. Over ten thousand magazines and journals are currently in print. Google, one of the largest Web search engines, currently searches over three billion Web pages. Walking into even an average-sized library and looking at all the books on the shelves can be overwhelming. Just as you will never be able to explore every nook and cranny on Earth, you will never be able to absorb all the accumulated knowledge of the human race.

The important thing is to be able to pinpoint the specific information that addresses your needs. Having read this book, I hope you will now be able to do this more efficiently, saving yourself lots of time and frustration so that you can more fully enjoy your time at college. If you get your research done more efficiently, as you should using the techniques I have described in this book, maybe you can reward yourself for a job well done by taking a real road trip.

Bon voyage!

Permissions

Academic Search Premier via EBSCO*host* © EBSCO Publishing. Reprinted with permission.

Dialog@CARL homepage © The Library Corp., Research Park, Inwood, WV 25428.
Reprinted with permission.

FirstSearch homepage © OCLC. Reprinted with permission. "FirstSearch" and "OCLC" are registered trademarks of OCLC Online Computer Library Center, Inc.

Google screens © Google, Inc. Reprinted with permission.

InfoTrac *Expanded Academic ASAP* © 2002 The Gale Group. Reprinted with permission.

ingenta homepage © 2002 ingenta, Inc. Reprinted with permission.

LexisNexis *Academic* © 2002 LexisNexis, a division of Reed Elsevier. All Rights Reserved.

Lycos screens © 2002 Lycos, Inc. All rights reserved. Lycos is a registered trademark of Carnegie Mellon University. Reprinted with permission.

"Moon" from "The Nine Planets Multimedia Tour" © William A. Arnett. Reprinted with permission.

netLibrary screenshot © 2001 - 2003, netLibrary, a division of OCLC Online Computer Library Center, Inc.. All rights reserved. Reprinted with permission.

Ovid's *Sociological Abstracts* © 2000-2003 Ovid Technologies, Inc. Reprinted with permission.

Image of *ProQuest General Reference* homepage produced by ProQuest Information and Learning Company. Inquiries may be made to: ProQuest Information and Learning Company, 300 North Zeeb Road, Ann Arbor, MI 48106-1346 USA. Telephone (734) 761-7400; E-mail: "mailto:info@il.proquest.com"; Web-page: "http://www.il.proquest .com". Reprinted with permission.

Reader's Guide to Periodical Literature © 1953 The H.W. Wilson Company. All rights reserved. Reprinted with permission.

SilverPlatter Webspirs version 4.3 © 1997-2000 SilverPlatter Information. Reprinted with permission.

WilsonWeb *BiographyPLUS* © 2002 The H.W. Wilson Company. All rights reserved. Reprinted with permission.

Yahoo! screens reproduced with permission of Yahoo! Inc. © 2000 by Yahoo! Inc. YAHOO! and the YAHOO! logo are trademarks of Yahoo! Inc.

Index

A

ABI/INFORM, 90
About.com, 129
*Academic American Ency-
   clopedia*, 51
Academic Search, 87, 107–
   109, 110
Accessible Archives, 76
accuracy (of sources), 146
addresses (Web), 126–127,
   144–145
AlltheWeb, 129
AltaVista, 129
AND (connecting term), 29–
   31, 113, 138
APA style, 148, 149
*Applied Science & Technol-
   ogy Index*, 90
Art Index, 90
articles, 7
   citation of, 150–152
   formats of, 76–77
   location of, 65–79
   obtaining, 75–79
Ask Jeeves, 129
atlases, 56–57
authority (of sources), 144–
   145
authors (searching by), 20–
   21

B

*Bartlett's Familiar Quota-
   tions*, 63
bibliographic databases, 84
bibliographies
   in articles, 66
   in books, 47
   book-length, 64
   compiling for paper, 148
biographical sources, 60–61
   organization of, 46–47
Biography Reference Bank,
   90
Biography Resource Center,
   87

Book Review Digest, 91
books, 5–7
  benefits of, 6
  citation of, 149–150
  organization of, 37–48
Boolean logic, 29–34
  use on Web, 138–140
Britannica, Encyclopaedia, 51, 52
broadening (a search), 110, 118
  see also OR (connecting term)
browsers (Web), 123–124
browsing, 5, 47
Business and Company Resource Center, 87
Business Periodicals Index, 91
Business Periodicals, ProQuest, 90
Business Source, 87

C

call numbers, 39
card catalogs, 28
  see also online catalogs
CD-ROMs, 81–83
Chicago Manual of Style, The, 148–149
chronological sources, 58–60
citations (article), 70
citations, bibliographic
  examples of, 149, 151, 152

citing
  books, 149–150
  electronic resources, 151–152
  periodicals, 150–151
  Web pages, 152–153
classification, 37–48
Collier's Encyclopedia, 51
connecting terms, 29–34
  combination of, 33–34
  use in Web searching, 138–140
  see also AND, NOT, OR
consortia, 11
Contemporary Authors, 61, 87
content (of sources), 145
cross references, 22–23, 27, 74, 115
currency (of sources), 146–147
Current Biography Yearbook, 61
CyberDewey, 38, 48

D

databases
  access to, 81–84, 106
  benefits of, 82–83
  definition of, 18
  searching of, 19–36, 110–118
  selection of, 81–103
  types of, 84
Dewey Decimal Classification, 39–42, 47–48

Dialog@CARL, 96–98
dictionaries, 55–56
Dictionary of American Biography, 61
Dictionary of Literary Biography, 61
directories, 62
directories (Web), 48, 133–136
documentation, 148–153
Dogpile, 129
domain names, 126

E

EBSCO*host*, 87–88
see also Academic Search
Education Index, 91
electronic books, 6–7, 98–99
electronic resources
citation of, 151–152
see also databases
Encarta Online, 52
Encyclopaedia Britannica, 51, 52
Encyclopedia Americana, 51
Encyclopedia of Associations, 62
encyclopedias
general, 51–52
subject-specific, 53–55
endnotes, 149
see also notes (documentation)
ERIC, 99
evaluation (of sources), 143–147

Expanded Academic ASAP, 68–72, 86–87, 107, 110–111, 114–117

F

Facts On File World News Digest, 59
fiction, 46
fields
in database records, 113–114
definition of, 18
searching within, 35–36
field-specific searching, 35–36, 113–117
FirstSearch, 92–93
footnotes, 149
see also notes (documentation)
full-image databases, 84
full-text databases, 84, 110–111, 112

G

General BusinessFile ASAP, 87
General Periodicals, ProQuest, 89
General Reference Center, 87
General Science Index, 91
Google, 129, 132–133, 139, 141
government sources, 58, 99–101, 125

GPO Monthly Catalog, 100
*Grolier's Multimedia Ency-
    clopedia*, 84

H

H. W. Wilson, 90–92
*Health and Wellness Re-
    source Center*, 87
Health Reference Center, 87
help
    asking for, 154–155
    online, 111
*Historical Newspapers,
    ProQuest*, 76–77, 90
homepages, 123
Humanities Index, 91
hypertext, 123, 127–128

I

ibid., 150
ILL, 11, 78–79
indexes
    back-of-book, 52–53, 67
    periodical, 9, 67–79
        electronic, 68–72
        print, 72–74
        purpose of, 65
        selection of, 74–75
    Web site, 52, 67
information technology
    changes in, 13–14
    limitations of, 12
InfoTrac, 68–72, 86–87
    *see also Expanded Aca-
        demic ASAP*

InfoTrac OneFile, 87
Ingenta, 101–102
interlibrary loan, 11, 78–79
Internet Explorer, 123–124
Internet. *See* World Wide Web

J

journals, 7
    authority of, 144
    characteristics of, 66–67
    citation of, 150–151
    limiting search to, 112

K

keyword searching, 28–36,
    54–55
    for articles, 108
    problems with, 34–35
keywords, 29

L

LexisNexis™ *Academic*, 93–
    94
Librarians' Index to the
    Internet, 129
libraries
    history of, 38–39
    and librarians, 10
    organization of, 37–48
    using other, 11, 78–79
Library of Congress, 42
Library of Congress Classifi-
    cation, 39, 42–47
*Library of Congress Subject
    Headings, The*, 24–28

limiters and limiting, 20, 112
links (Web), 123
Lycos, 129, 131–132, 139

M

magazines, 7
    characteristics of, 66–67
    citation of, 150–151
Manual for Writers of Term Papers, Theses, and Dissertations, A (Turabian), 148
MasterFILE, 87
Medline, 99
MetaCrawler, 129
metasearch engines, 142
microfilm, 76
MLA Style, 148, 149
multimedia databases, 84

N

narrowing (a search), 112–118
    see also AND; NOT
natural language searching, 109–110, 139–140
NetFirst, 92–93
netLibrary, 6, 98–99
Netscape, 123–124
Newspaper Abstracts, ProQuest, 89
Newspaper Source, 88
newspapers, 7
    indexes for, 88, 89–90, 93–94, 97

NOT (connecting term), 33, 113, 138
notes (documentation), 148–149
    examples of, 150, 151, 152

O

OmniFile, 92
online catalogs, 9, 17–36
online databases. *See* databases
online services
    databases provided by, 85–86
    structure of, 106
Open Directory, 130
OR (connecting term), 31, 111, 138–139
Ovid, 95–96

P

parenthetical citations, 149
Periodical Abstracts, 89
periodicals, 7
    citation of, 150–151
    indexing of. *See* indexes, periodical
    organization of, 77–78
    types of, 66–67
    see also articles
planning (research), 4–12
popularity ranking, 141
portal sites, 132
primary sources, 66

Project Gutenberg, 6
PROMPT, 87
ProQuest, 89–90
proximity operators, 113
Publication Manual of the American Psychological Association, The, 148

Q

quotations (sources of), 63–64

R

Reader's Guide to Periodical Literature, 73–74, 91–92
records, 18, 113–114
"red books," 24–26
reference sources, 49–64
relevancy ranking, 141
research
guidelines, 153–155
planning, 4–12
resources. *See* sources

S

"scavenger hunts," 49
scholarly journals." *See* journals
Scribner Encyclopedia of American Lives, 61
search engines, 9–10, 93, 102, 129–142
and ranking results, 140–141
scope of, 136–137

selection of, 141–142
searching
by author, 20–21
by keyword, 28–36, 54–55, 108
natural language, 109–110, 139–140
by subject, 21–28, 114–115, 118
by title, 20–21
secondary sources, 66
SilverPlatter, 95–96
Social Sciences Index, 92
sources
citation of, 148–153
evaluation of, 143–147
learning to use, 10
location of, 8–11
selection of, 14
types of, 5–8
spiders (Web), 137
Statistical Abstract of the United States, 57
statistical sources, 57–58
stopwords, 29
subheadings, 23
subject headings, 24–28, 107–109
subject searching, 21–28
for articles, 114–115, 118
benefits of, 21
"surfing" (Web), 127–128

T

time management, 11–12
timelines, 59–60

Timelines of History, 60
titles (searching by), 20–21
topic selection, 1–4, 21
top-level domains, 126, 144
tours, 10
trade journals, 66
truncation, 32–33, 111, 139

U

UnCover, 101–102
uniform resource locators, 126–127, 144–145
United States Government Manual, 62
URLs, 126–127, 144–145

W

Web. *See* World Wide Web
Web pages
   citation of, 152–153
   length of, 123
   vs. Web sites, 153
Web sites, 8
   authority of, 144–145
   corporate, 124
   directories of, 48, 133–136
   educational, 124–125
   evaluation of, 8, 50, 83–84, 146, 147
   governmental, 99–101, 125

   indexing of, 52, 67
   location of, 9–10
   nonprofit, 124
   personal, 125
   ranking of, 140–141
   vs. Web pages, 153
WebCrawler, 130
Who's Who, 60, 62
Wilson Biographies Plus, 90
Wilson Business Abstracts, 91
Wilson, H. W., 90–92
World Almanac and Book of Facts, 58
World Book Encyclopedia, 51
World Wide Web, 121–142
   advertising on, 83
   content of, 124–125
   finding information on, 126–142
   history of, 121–122
   organization of, 48
   problems with, 122
   searching of, 137–140
      see also search engines
   "surfing" of, 127, 128
   structure of, 123–124
WorldCat, 92–93, 130, 133
WWW Virtual Library, 130

Y

Yahoo!, 130, 133–136